ADVANCED ENERGY

HEALING THEORY AND TECHNIQUE
FOR REIKI AND EMPATHIC HEALERS

D1571042

Published by Mindstir Media, LLC
45 Lafayette Rd | Suite 181| North Hampton, NH 03862 | USA
1.800.767.0531 | www.mindstirmedia.com

Printed in the United States of America
ISBN-13: 978-0-9991507-5-7
Library of Congress Control Number: 2017953183

ADVANCED ENERGY

HEALING THEORY AND TECHNIQUE
FOR REIKI AND EMPATHIC HEALERS

JIM HANSEN, REIKI MASTER

MINDSTIR MEDIA

DEDICATION

Dedicated to my wife Pat for her constant encouragement and love.

ACKNOWLEDGEMENTS

With thanks to Bill Stucky, Reiki Master who introduced me to Reiki, Bill Burns who carefully guided my studies, Jack and Kathy Fellman who read and critiqued the manuscript as it developed, the South Tyrol Museum of Archaeology who provided photos of Otzi the Iceman, and Brian McMorrow who provided the photo of Amenhotep III taken at the Temple of Luxor. Einstein quotes were taken from various sources on the web. Illustrations were drawn by Judy Krassowski. Last and certainly not the least, Pat Hansen who read, reread and helped edit the manuscript as it grew.

A human being is a part of the whole, called by us "Universe", a part limited in time and space. He experiences himself, his thoughts and feelings as something separated from the rest — a kind of optical delusion of his consciousness. This delusion is a kind of prison for us...

—Albert Einstein

TABLE OF CONTENTS

Energy healing is as old as humanity itself. Earliest records of it and near-modern medical treatments date to Egypt 4,000 years ago where it is shown in temple wall carvings and a few very fragile parchment rolls. The earliest known written mention of acupuncture efforts are slightly older, coming from Chinese literature 4,500 years ago. Reiki as a practice came on the scene much more recently, starting in the late 1800s.

The human nonphysical anatomy consists of various energy centers and channels, nonphysical bodies overlaying the physical body and various control mechanisms. The roles played by the chakras and their relationship between the physical and nonphysical bodies are explored as they apply to healing technique. We analyze energy flow and its relationship to the mind, and of its influence on the emotional structure of the human consciousness.

CHAPTER 3 – ENERGY AND CONSCIOUSNESS 63

Here we establish a working set of descriptions and definitions for energy and consciousness, as well as for other metaphysical terms used in this book. These concepts allow a more focused and methodical exploration of the energy healing techniques described.

Chapter 4 – Healing Theory and Practice 93

Healing is the removal of restriction—or in metaphysical terminology, resistance. As advanced healers, we do not attempt to diagnose the cause of a restriction. Rather, we send healing energy to assist in accomplishing an associated life learning lesson. Once the learning has been accomplished, the restriction dissolves away and healing at the physical level takes place.

The fundamental energy concept that helps with this process is intent driven. There are four basic forms of healing energy that can be supplied by the healer either for personal use or to heal others. These are insight, perspective, reinforcement and support.

We conclude this chapter with an introduction to crystal technology.

CHAPTER 5 – REIKI AND MINERAL MACHINES

Everyone working as an energy healer is sensitive in one way or another to energy flow and has a baseline or minimum sensitivity to that flow. At the highest level, sensitivity is established as an incarnational matter prior to birth, indicating its relevance to one's incarnational plan. Here we describe various methods of sending energy to those we heal without physical contact.

FOREWORD

This project is based on my original Reiki Master's thesis. It took some time before any real motivation to make it into a publishable work arrived. By late summer 2016 the project became somewhat presentable. Since then it has been a work in progress, and the final result is this book of history, theory, and applied healing technique.

The theories on sickness, illness, and energy outlined in this book represent a fundamental departure from most of energy healing. No traditional energy healing practice attempts to define or describe the fundamental process that enables their healing art to work. Instead, most either ignore any attempt to understand the true nature of what happens when a healing takes place, or rely on the sweeping mystical assertions of others to explain it.

Once the principles behind the healing art are exposed, new ways of manipulating the process become apparent. Some of those possibilities are presented in this book. With this new understanding, many of the mystical healing practices described since the time of the ancient Egyptians suddenly make sense as we see how underlying intent works. Perhaps most profoundly, the healer is no longer asked to accept healing ability as an article of faith and healings as miracles. The effects evolved through techniques described here are demonstrable and have proven more efficacious than strictly traditional healing approaches.

This book makes a concerted attempt to explain that there is a recognizable, common connection between the physical world we all live in and the nonphysical, one that most healers can learn to ultimately sense and manipulate. This is first and foremost a book about the manipulation of consciousness. As such, it describes concepts and practical techniques that differ substantially with traditional or mystical explanations of energy healing. These are not untested, unproven ideas. They are based on empirical discoveries that have been incorporated and taught as a part of my Reiki classes conducted over many years. You are invited, through this book, to try these techniques for yourself.

Although nearly everyone with an interest in energy healing can benefit from this book, those with formal training in Reiki 1 and Reiki 2 or other energy healing techniques will find it of particular interest.

Nonphysical healing and related phenomena cannot be accurately described using purely physical terms. Matters of nonphysical practice are entirely subjective because they consist only of potential and concept. Thus we have no language to explicitly describe what those working in this field manipulate or experience.

Indeed, the language of nonphysical healing is one of metaphor, allegory, and parable combined with sensations and feelings that sometimes have no physical description. This often drives those of an analytical, technical, or scientific bent away from the field, which is unfortunate.

Before going further, it is important that you take the time to understand the intended meanings of some of the words used. I use nonphysical and metaphysical to refer to aspects of pure consciousness, as opposed to the physical world where we lead our daily lives.

The term nonphysical is also used to describe the intangible parts of the body, as well as other such effects including pure energy and consciousness. Things of the physical are those that can be observed through one or more of our five senses or by their extension through scientific instrumentation.

In order to avoid confusion, the term "higher power" refers to the spiritual essence of which we are a part. Many higher powers are "too large" to fit the human form, and so a part of it remains in the nonphysical realm. That part of the higher power that does fit the human mold is called our "higher self." It is the higher self that religions call our "soul."

Completing this line of thought, your personal reality space, which exists in the moment, externally consists of only those things that are sensed by your five senses. Everything else you find in it is unreal and cannot, in the moment, either help or harm you.

A few words about the term "learning experience" are also in order. Spiritual or nonphysical growth is based on the accumulation of experience and thereby perspective. It is the acquisition of perspective that is termed a "learning experience." As a pure consciousness, our collection of accumulated experience and perspective is what makes us who and what we really are.

The purpose of living a physical life, our "earth experience," is to allow narrowly focused living through a specific set of learning experiences. These experiences are accomplished through a series of restrictions formed that comply with our incarnational plan established by us, our higher self and higher power prior to birth. At the level of this discussion, the human consciousness and its rational mind form the first (or primary) restriction, and the body with its limited arsenal of physical talents, abilities, and senses refines and refocuses these limitations to the precise area of the learning desired.

Typically, the first third of our lives is spent accumulating memory passed down by parents and society and learning a skill set usually based on our natural talents and abilities. The part of civilization into which we are born forms the cultural context to be used as the framework of our present life. In this way, we do not waste time by personally having to re-experience all of history—which would be practically impossible—as we grow up.

We unconsciously use this knowledge to guide and build our lives, usually without thinking of it as being restrictive. This leaves us time to spend the majority of our lives focused on those aspects of life we came to experience and learn as a spiritual means of growth. Life learning experiences are collected as we expose, uncover and develop new talents and abilities. This further releases restriction, and life expands in new and exciting ways. At least, this is the way life is supposed to work.

Illness (which includes sickness, a biological or physiological condition of the body) is the term used to describe a profound restriction of any kind that narrows focus, thus directing us and our expression in some way. We define the lifting of such restrictions as healing. Healing occurs by learning through life experience or by receiving insight at a particular level of consciousness, sometimes from a healer.

At death, our mind, memory, and acquired knowledge die with the brain, but remnants of it are retained by the more physical aspects of our nonphysical bodies for some time. From the nonphysical perspective, our human consciousness retains only the experiences acquired during this lifetime. It is these aspects of self that psychics and mediums can contact, but only for a relatively short period of time after death. What happens before birth and after death is a subject area not covered in this book.

The esoteric nature of energy healing and the descriptions of technique that follow defy logic. To my knowledge, the integrated healing techniques, their broad application in such general terms to life, and much of the background material presented in the pages that follow have not been previously published.

Test. Modify. Apply. These are the things that you must do in order to grow as a healer. Virtually everything in the nonphysical, even conscious awareness itself, is subjective to the individual. Successful understanding of these concepts can only arrive after all of your preconceived and cherished notions are set aside, and you test them for yourself.

As you do this, trust yourself, your intuition, and what you experience at the time as being real. For by the very next day, your mind will surely attempt to add its own twist, its own version, its own denial of the reality that you experienced less than twenty-four hours before. Trust in self is all important.

This is not an armchair book. It is meant to serve as an active guide for your personal exploration into the nonphysical part of yourself, not as a set of fossilized facts or fanciful techniques. If it contains truth for you, that truth will withstand your testing, resting exclusively on its own merit.

It is vitally important that you, as a healer, explore, challenge, and verify everything in this book to find its ultimate usefulness for you. Otherwise, it will become just another book of concepts sitting like a trophy on your bookshelf. Always remember that good instincts tell you what to do long before your mind has figured it out. As you uncover truth as it applies to you, your confidence in yourself and your healing skills will increase. And with that, you will discover the healing that will ultimately set you free.

Jim Hansen
2017

CHAPTER 1

INTRODUCTION TO NONPHYSICAL HEALING

How strange is the lot of us mortals! Each of us is here for a brief sojourn, for what purpose we know not, though sometimes sense it. But we know from daily life that we exist for other people first of all for whose smiles and well-being our own happiness depends.
— Albert Einstein

This chapter introduces a new interpretation of healing, how it works, and its relationship to daily life. Energy healing is the nonphysical art of bringing new energy into the body, manipulating what is already available, or expelling it. The request most often made to healers is for the sick and injured to be made whole, but the healing art extends much further than that. Healing, as it will be described later, involves the entire human condition: the body, mind, psyche, and environment.

And so a distinction must be drawn between types of affliction. Sickness is the term used to describe some undesired physical or mental situation related to the body, and illness describes a condition in the general human condition. People who ask for a healing in either category do so because they desire, and agree to accept, change. And so, we arrive at the root definition of a healer. Healers of every persuasion serve those who come to them by effecting a change in their lives.

Although the history of the healing art is long, the archeological record of it is short, and written documentation of it is rare. Because the practice is so ancient, much of the early healing arts are shrouded in myth, legend, and perhaps a touch of fantasy. But occasionally a dramatic find, such as Otzi the Iceman found in the Tyrolean Alps along the border between Austria and Italy, provides new physical evidence of early energy healing techniques.

Difficult to define, the spiritual sense of ourselves from which energy healing is derived is usually associated in some way to personal survival prior to and after death. Our rational senses, on the other hand, deny this. The essence of an unseen and thereby unknowable realm is rationally and logically declared not to exist since no physical evidence of it can be found. Despite the strength of rational thought, we are still convinced, still believe, that there is a spiritual side to ourselves.

There is a distinct difference between healers and physicians. Healers do not question the spiritual nature of their art or the extent of what it can do. Physicians, on the other hand, limit themselves to dispensing potions prepared to narrowly target defined physical and mental issues confronting their patients. As a rule, physicians limit themselves to healing bodies and minds with little or no training in spiritual matters or other core issues important to those who come to them. This reveals two important limitations of the practicing physician.

First, a proper diagnosis must be made before medication can be prescribed. This is because the philosophy of modem medical art insists that sickness is the result of a single pathogen (or pathogens), chemistry, or other physical condition that has gone awry. Thus it is reasoned that a single potion or procedure should be able to kill the offending bugs or correct the other imbalances within the body.

The second limitation follows this, in that, the array of modern medicines available today are essentially single-purpose potions. That is, each medication or other medical treatment is effective for only a few sicknesses or particular aspects of them. It is, therefore, very important that the physician correctly identify the affliction before prescribing a cure.

Healers, energy healers, in particular, do not diagnose or prescribe other than to ask the body, soul, or psyche to agree to be healed. The energy then given is adjusted to heal at the level that best serves the interests of the sick, regardless of the affliction.

Although the goals of healers and physicians are identical, an undeniable schism separates the two healing art forms. It is not one of essential ability or technique. Each side has a multitude of successful physical and alternative philosophical approaches.

At its very root, the gulf separating healers and Western medicine is that of our rational thoughts and mind in competition with our intuitive sense of self of the heart.

Western medical practice is the product of rational thought and reason, a particular and very special mode of thought which the human race, as a whole, did not exercise until fairly recent times, perhaps starting in earnest about 4,500 years ago. On the other hand, the art of healing is handed down from times when the human condition was ruled by unseen gods and nature itself, long before the rational mind invaded our thought modality.

Healing practices are the product of innate or intuitive understanding of our nonphysical nature. Medical science, on the other hand, is the result of the rational thought process, that of logic, deduction, and reasoning.

Rational thought, involved only with physical processes, is intrinsically incapable of dealing with undefinable matters and tries to deny intuitive solutions. Intuitive thought is not logical. It accepts the final solution as a matter of insight and cares not about the details or steps taken along the way to discovery. As different as oil and water, intuitive and rational thought are the two distinctly different interpretive processes that present reality to modern man.

As persuasive as rational arguments are, we as complex beings are not quite ready to entirely abandon our intuitive outlook on life. Indeed, nearly half of our brain seems primarily devoted to matters of spiritual, the nonphysical and metaphysical sides of our nature. Whether this is actually so is a matter of interpretation of the evidence, but there is a difference in the way each hemisphere processes information from our surrounding environment. The left seems ordered to do it sequentially, the right side in a simultaneous or parallel fashion.

No matter how intuitive we may be, today's modern human is forced to confront matters of the nonphysical and our spiritual nature primarily with our rationality. It takes no small amount of courage to overcome fear before many can ask for nonphysical healings. And it takes even greater courage for those with a calling to heal to accept the risk that accompanies their destiny.

The History of Healing

Although healers and the healing arts have been around as long as the human condition has existed, relatively little is recorded through the eyes of a modern healer. The scholarly appraisal of "primitive" medical practices is generally one of low regard. Viewed principally as superstition coupled with supplication and appeasement of unseen gods or spirits, it has taken Western medicine until the late 1950s to start looking at the herbal cures of the Indian Ayurvedic, Chinese traditional medicine, and those of our remaining indigenous cultures as sources of new healing compounds.

The historical record of healing is a long one, but of particular interest to energy healers are acupuncture and the various healing practices of ancient Egypt which include both Reiki-like energy healing as well as a substantial traditional medical practice.

The Origins of Medical Science

Western medicine has its roots in fifth century BCE Greece. Hippocrates, who died somewhere between 377 and 359 BCE, is considered its "father," but well-grounded scientific medical practices can be traced further back. About a hundred years earlier, the Pythagorean School at Crotona produced the most famous Greek physicians, among them Alcmaeon, who is often called the "real" father of Greek medicine. His recorded contributions from incomplete records include the discovery of the optic nerve, eustachian tubes, recognition of the brain as the central organ of thought and an explanation of the physiology of sleep.

The Egyptians about 4,500 years ago left traces that their medical system went far beyond any of the Greek practices, and was more in line with present-day medicine than most realize. This evidence is brought to light by the Edwin Smith Surgical Papyrus, named after the American Egyptologist who bought it in 1862 from an antiquities dealer in Egypt. Translation of this document waited until 1930 when it was discovered to be a medical treatise written with a modern structure and with the same general organizational scheme as *Gray's Anatomy*, a universally used text in today's medical schools.

This papyrus describes forty-eight traumatic cases starting with the head and working down the body. The text consists of a concise diagnosis followed by the recommended treatment and the probable outcomes. All are described in dispassionate, clinical terms. Prescribed treatments include the first use of sutures to close wounds, bandaging with honey (a bactericide) to prevent infection, splinting, and many other modern treatments. Only one case mentions the use of magical charms as a means to promote healing.

This document, dated to about 1550 BCE, is the world's earliest known medical treatise, but unfortunately, it is an incomplete copy of an earlier original, ending in mid-sentence. Based on the language and style used in the treatise, the original from which it was copied is thought to date between roughly 2500–3000 BCE.

Physical evidence of the medical practices described in this papyrus has been discovered in the remains of workers buried near the Stepped Pyramid, built for Djoser (2667–2648 BCE) of the Third Dynasty. Healed leg bones following amputation show expert medical care, and there is clear evidence of broken bones being healed after splinting. This site also revealed evidence of the earliest known brain surgery showing, a skull that had been cut away in several locations to remove internal pressure caused by a cancerous brain tumor.

The Surgical Papyrus is obviously the product of a mature medical science, based on observation and reason. Given that the original is of the 2500 BCE era, it clearly demonstrates that rational human thought was possible even at this early date. Nothing in classical Greek medicine that followed some 2,200 years later compares to this achievement, and it took modern medicine an additional 2,000 years before it recovered this knowledge and incorporated it into common practice.

It is generally thought, but certainly not proven, that the author of the Surgical Papyrus was Imhotep, probably the world's first multi-genius. He held many high titles in service to the Pharaoh and was an architect, philosopher, poet, and, more importantly for us, a physician. His reputation was so great that for nearly 3,000 years, until the Christian revolution stopped the practice, pilgrims seeking healings traveled from throughout the Middle East to leave votives at shrines in his honor. (Great caution and care should be used when searching the web for *authentic* information on the Surgical Papyrus.)

OTZI THE ICEMAN

Acupuncture is the art of manipulating the existing energy flow and balance within the body. The understanding of the complex energy flows in the human body appear to be much older than the medical systems practiced in both ancient India and China. Otzi is the mummified remains of a fifty-year-old male who died after being shot in the back with an arrow around 3300 BCE.

He was subsequently frozen in a glacier where his corpse remained untouched until it was discovered along the Austrian-Italian border by hikers in 1991. Fully intact, this person came through to us, not as a ceremonially buried figure, but just as he was, complete with everything that he carried at the moment of his death. He has been the subject of intense scientific study ever since.

Interestingly for us, it appears that he was being treated for arthritis using what we call acupuncture, and that it was applied in exactly the same manner as it is done now. He also has the earliest known tattoos, some sixty-one of them, many of which are placed along the acupuncture urinary-bladder channel for treating lower back pain.

His tattoos are nondecorative, and most consist of parallel lines on his back and other acupuncture locations related to pain. A simple cross is on his ankle at the master point for back pain. There is no doubt of their placement in relation to the acupuncture sites in use today.

X-rays, CT scans, and other diagnostics show that the Iceman must have lived with considerable pain with arthritic conditions in his lower back, hip, knee, and ankle, thus indicating that the tattooing was not performed by chance. Tattooing is known in virtually all cultures throughout the world. Many of them have developed tattooing at acupuncture locations as a way to provide constant activation of those sites.

ACUPUNCTURE IN CHINA

Probably the earliest written records describing acupuncture are found in the Nei Hing Su Wen also known as Huang Ti's (2697-2579 BCE) largely philosophical text, *The Yellow Emperor's Classic of Internal Medicine*. Here "bian" stones (needles of sharpened stone) were used.

Eventually, metal needles developed into the classic "nine needles" of which the filiform remains in use today. The other eight needles slowly evolved into modern surgical instruments.

There is a question whether Huang Ti, the near-mythological founder of the Chinese civilization, actually existed. Some historians further doubt that he wrote the Nei Hing Su Wen, which some date as recently as 475-221 BCE.

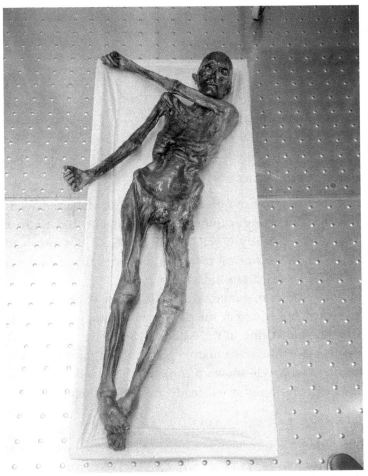

Photo 1-1 Iceman's photos courtesy and (c) South Tyrol Museum of Archaeology/ www.iceman.it

Photo 1-2, Photo 1-3 The majority of Otzi's tattoos are in the form of a cross or parallel lines. Many of them are located on acupuncture meridians for treating lower back pain.

ACUPUNCTURE WORLDWIDE

So far, there has been no historical or anthropological evidence that shows a thread connecting acupuncture development, and it now appears that it was independently developed in scattered locations across the globe, with the only historical record of its development into a formalized practice being that from India and China.

The Iceman shows that a broad understanding of energy flow within the body must have existed at the time of his death, just 200 years after the earliest known writing in the Middle East evolved. He also demonstrates that acupuncture was a mature practice, and that tattooing of acupuncture sites was a well-known technique, this about a thousand years before the first mention of it was made in Chinese literature.

EGYPTIAN ENERGY HEALING

The first energy healing system similar to Reiki energy healing appears to have originated in Egypt. The early Egyptian term for Ki, Sa, is translated as "life energy" and "magical fluid." Early in their prehistory, the Egyptians developed a thorough understanding of life energy and learned to manipulate it to improve health and for various other purposes. What these other "purposes" were, we have been left with no clear idea.

When trying to understand the energy healing practices of the Egyptians, it is important to recognize the essential philosophical doctrine under which it was performed. Their concept of the practice was that life energy was drawn by the gods from the Lake of Sa, which was thought to be located in the northern sky. The gods gave it both to themselves and to humanity.

The meaning of this is more clear when we understand that the Egyptians held that the heavens (stars) were separated from the earth by "waters." Therefore, the "lake (or pond) of Sa" refers to the universe as a cosmic or spiritual source for the energy. This may account for some of the intense astronomical interest held by the Egyptians, and more specifically, to the polar stars. (We have experienced many different "north pole" stars over the course of the 25,735-year period of the earth's precessional rotation.)

But even this concept may be more literal than the Egyptians understood it to be. Ancient Egyptian thought, for the most part, was pre-rational. Their thinking was based on concept far more than present day rational thinking, which is largely driven by comparison and duality. It is entirely possible that the Egyptian gods themselves were envisioned by the initiated as various forms of energy, and that their interaction with humanity was essentially one of energy transference in one form or another. In any event, the Egyptians understood and used transference of energy as an ordinary, accepted healing practice.

To the Egyptians, Sa was what we call today vital energy, prana, chi, or life energy. As a matter of comment, the basis of all the greater mysteries of Egypt, Babylonia, Sumeria and Greece can conclusively be traced to the Egyptian concept of energy and its manipulation. The energy was used primarily for transforming consciousness, healing, and magik. All were major temple preoccupations in ancient Egypt and formed the basis of what is known today as energy healing and Ritual Magik. To the initiated Egyptian temple priests, the application was unimportant; it was all the same energy at play.

The Egyptian belief was that this cosmic source of energy could be

ACUPUNCTURE AND CHINESE MEDICINE

The energy manipulation modalities exemplified by the Chinese and Indian traditions are distinctive. The approaches developed in India describe and work with internal human energy sources, namely the chakras and other nonphysical aspects of our being. Chinese acupuncture manipulates the energy already flowing throughout the body along its various internal pathways.

Until the discovery of Otzi the Iceman, acupuncture was thought to have originated in China. This is presently in doubt. Even so, China offers the first written word on the subject, *The Yi Jing (Book of Changes)*. This 1122 BCE text mentions the three natural energies of Qi, paving the way for Qigong to eventually evolve into an energy healing system in its own right.

Even earlier, the Huang Di Nei Jing, *The Yellow Emperor's Internal Medicine Classic*, was compiled by the "mystical" author Huang Di, the Yellow Emperor (circ. 2697 BCE). It consists of eighty-one treatises with the latest recorded around 200 BCE, depending on the source. An ancient text, it probably predates its author or editor. This text mentions the use of Bian Shi, or stone probes, used to adjust Qi circulation during the reign of the Yellow Emperor, but does not describe their use or mention acupuncture specifically. The Nei Jing, coming much later, reveals basic acupuncture theory as well as healing philosophy and principles, thus providing the foundation for traditional Chinese medicine that is still in use today.

Acupuncture is one of the few "energy" healing systems that have been embraced by mainstream Western medicine, although relatively few physicians have been certified. In the United States, acupuncture is largely practiced in private clinics.

drawn down by adepts and tapped for the physical benefit of ordinary people. Sa could also be transmitted between individuals by the laying on of the hands. When the gods themselves eventually exhausted their personal supply of Sa, they periodically returned to the northern skies to replenish it from the mysterious "pond of Sa." Sa was also said to be circulated among their gods. Gaston Maspero, a well-known and respected Egyptologist of the late 1800s and early twentieth century, writing about the Egyptian gods, said:

> *"They were not all equally charged with it (Sa); some had more, others less, their energy being in proportion to the amount which they contained. The better supplied willingly gave of the superfluity to those who lacked it, and all could readily transmit it to mankind, this transfusion being easily accomplished in the temples."*

One of the priestly duties of the temple priest-astronomers was the "imposition of Sa" which was given to all who came to the temples and asked for it. Although the priests could transmit it themselves, Sa could also be stored in and dispensed on demand by the statues of the gods:

> *"The king or any ordinary man who wished to be impregnated (or given a transfusion of Sa), presented himself before the statue of the god, and squatted at its feet with his back to the statue. The statue then placed its right hand on the nape of his neck, and by making passes caused the fluid to flow from it and to accumulate in him as a receiver. This rite was of temporary efficacy only, and required frequent renewal in order that its benefit might be maintained."*

Giving Sa to mortals "depleted" the god's personal supply:

> *"By using or transmitting it the gods themselves exhausted their Sa of life; and the less vigorous replenished themselves from the stronger, while the latter went to draw fresh fullness from a mysterious pond in the northern sky, called the pond of Sa."*

Around 1350 BCE, Amenhotep III built the Temple of Luxor and in it is a bas-relief carving showing the "imposition" of Sa from the god Amun-Ra, using the posture just described. This is probably the earliest known ancient physical evidence showing "energy healing" similar to Reiki as a mature practice. Maspero's writing indicates that there were "many" papyri in existence discussing energy, healing, and magik. Unfortunately, his sources are given in French, and now being over a hundred years old, it is difficult to trace or access these citations in English.

This engraving does not date the start of energy healing. Indeed, by the time it was made, the art was a very mature practice. How old energy healing really is, we'll probably never know. The Greek historian Herodotus reported that Egyptians told him that they were the third civilization to live in Africa and claimed to have records going back more than two of the "great years," meaning two complete cycles of the precessional periods, something on the order of 52,000 years. Though many of Herodotus's claims are inaccurate, this account does indicate something of the Egyptian antiquity.

Egyptian history is much older than that indicated by the Table of Abydos, which lists some sixty-five kings, from Menes, founder of the dynastic line of succession, through the end of the Twelfth Dynasty. Assuming normal lifetimes of about three generations per century, Egyptologists conclude this could mean that this line of monarchs spanned about 2,166 years. There are gaps in the table between the Twelfth and Eighteenth Dynasties, and in any event, dates recorded before the table, whether written in stone or on papyrus, are based on celestial chronology and in cycles of astronomical time, both of which are subject to interpretation.

Probably the most valuable documentation of Egypt's lengthy past is recorded on the Royal Papyrus of Turin which gives a complete listing of the kings reigning over both Upper and Lower Egypt extending from Menes to the New Empire. It mentions nine dynasties including the venerables (civilizations prior to the dynastic Egyptian era) of Memphis, North, and the Shemsu-Hor, usually translated as the "Companions of Horace."

This document, whose last two lines remained nearly intact, gives "venerables Shemsu-Hor, 13,420 years" and "Reigns up to Shemsu-Hor, 23,200 years." Together, this indicates that Egyptian history began some 36,620 years before Menes. Little of this papyrus remains readable as it was destroyed while being carted off to Italy.

Today virtually nothing remains of those prior civilizations which represent Egypt's lengthy legacy. The desert sands have wiped away nearly

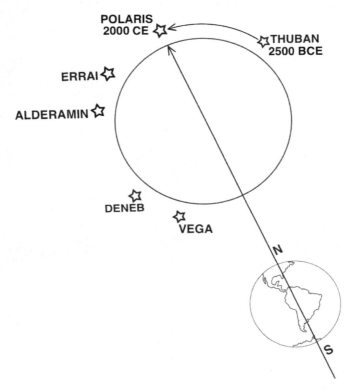

Drawing 1-1 Precession of the Equinoxes. The earth swings around like a top as it gradually slows down over the eons. This causes the north pole star to change from Polaris (at present) to other stars as shown. It takes something over 25,735 years to complete one "wobble." The star Thuban was the North Star at the time the pyramids were constructed, some 4,500 years ago.

every trace of the old ones, and the Christian-inspired suppression of the pagan temples and clerics, not to mention the burning of the Library at Alexandria, destroyed any chance that we're likely to discover significantly more about this fascinating aspect of their culture anytime soon.

The uninitiated majority of the ancient Egyptian population understood the Egyptian astronomy and life energy in terms of parable, metaphor, and myths. Without the interpretive knowledge of the initiated, that is, innate knowledge, the myths have to be interpreted literally. Thus

Photo 1-4 The coronation of Amenhotep III (approximately 1386–1349 BCE) by the god Amun-Ra. Amun-Ra is providing Amenhotep III Sa as a part of his coronation ceremony. This is the oldest known image of energy projection. Photo courtesy Brian McMorrow, www.pbase.com/bmcmorrow.

the mythology of Greece and Rome, based on that of the Egyptians, was passed along in literal form. Under new and different names, Egyptian myths formed the basis of most ancient pagan beliefs and practices throughout the ancient world, propagating into every culture and religion.

The true and often astronomical knowledge coded in these myths was the province of only the initiated. It and the basis of Egypt's esoteric knowledge was fatally carried down in an oral, not written, tradition. With the possible exception of Pythagoras, and one or two other Greeks, these truths remained hidden with the Egyptian priests, and behind the parables, until it was completely lost as the temples were closed or destroyed, all accessible records burned on pain of death, and the intelligentsia killed and dispersed.

And so it was that the priests in ancient Egypt were probably the first energy healers.

REIKI DEFINED

That traditional Usui Reiki as it is practiced today was formalized in Japan during the late 1800s is not in question. The historical record of this aspect of its development has been explored in several books, notably those of Frank Arjava Petter and William Lee Rand.

It has been suggested that energy healing practices similar to Reiki originally came through China from Tibet and India, with the earliest traces of it in Assyria. Independent and reliable sources for this information are difficult to find. However, evidence is available, particularly from India, where there are many conceptual identities in terminology and practice. Indeed, Reiki, as a practice, is currently widespread in India, but there, like in the Western World, it suffers from a plethora of variants and imitative practices.

The term Reiki, composed of the two words *Rei* and *Ki*, is of Japanese origin. The first word, *Rei*, refers to spirit or "spiritual" in a general sense. Conceptually, it is the "vehicle" which carries the energy itself, the Ki. As a spiritual concept, *Ki* is found in many cultures. In China, it is *Qi* or *Chi*, and in India, it is *Prana*, or in Yoga terms, *Shakti*. *Ki* refers to the infinite energy available through our spiritual heritage, our higher self, our god, or the "universe." Terms with identical meanings are found in all cultures throughout the world.

Putting these two words together, we understand the meaning more clearly as "energy through our spiritual essence or channel." This is the derivation of Reiki as a concept of life energy or spiritual power. It is nonphysical in nature, and as such, intangible except for the effects it has on those giving and receiving it. Being an energy from our higher spiritual source means that it has a broad and general application to every aspect of life.

THE NONPHYSICAL WORLD

The study of advanced energy healing technique inevitably requires a new and usually different perspective on life as a part of its practice and philosophy. When the nonphysical world of pure consciousness is viewed as our "normal" state, a new awareness gradually emerges of the purpose of life, what sickness and healing actually are, and how they relate to life.

The nonphysical is a realm of concept and potential only. We briefly draw on it when we design and create. Thus, it is a nearly constant source of inspiration accessible at will. We briefly enter the nonphysical whenever our conscious awareness shifts from physical matters, as reported by our five senses. Being in a thoughtless meditative state is a very natural state of being, but for the most part, it is one that is removed from our normal awareness.

Because spirituality and energy healing are nonphysical in nature, the discussion, study, and comprehension of this aspect of life from the physical perspective is difficult. We have no language to describe the nonphysical because we, as physical beings, base all of our rational logic and thought on physical conceptualizations that involve time and space. Even so, in many ways, the nonphysical is reflected into the physical. Probably the most obvious mandate applying to both the physical and nonphysical is that of growth. In both realms, it is either grow or (eventually) perish.

This is manifest in the physical as the will to survive and pervades all cultures and all species of life. The willingness to change and adapt to the environment is the key to survival, and thus a willingness to change is necessary before growth can take place. Because our institutions, organizations, governments and even civilizations reflect the sum total of their spiritual constituency, this primal imperative applies to them as well.

The only activities and life experiences that give us genuine satisfaction and a sense of fulfillment are those that include creativity, growth, or exploration as a major component. "I gave birth and created a family." "I traveled and saw the wonders of the world and all its people." "I planted crops and watched them feed the world." "I built an industry, a community, a city, a nation." "I taught people and saw them grow and mature." "I grew strong and developed into a fine athlete." "I entertained people and made them laugh." "I healed people and made them whole again." These statements are self-reflective and evidence of our conscious recognition of who we are and what we have become. With reflection, this takes place for everyone, regardless of their particular station in life.

Although there are many other means to achieve spiritual growth, the physical world we know, the earth experience, was chosen by each of us prior to birth because of its particular environment. Here, human consciousness explores itself through tightly focused physical awareness. Conscious awareness is artificially constrained through a system of restrictions so that a detailed and very specific study of particular aspects of self can take place.

In the broadest definition, a restriction is anything that prevents the experience or living of life in a way not totally reflective of who and what we as individuals actually are. In the mental or psychological sense, restrictions are caused by the denial of our true identity thus fostering a false sense of who we are. As self-doubt grows, fear of several varieties spring up, and we start living in the shadow of authority figures, where life revolves around pleasing them, not ourselves.

Restrictions are not always of a mental nature. Carl Jung's concept of synchronicity is an attempt to explain why things seem to happen at the time they do. For example, why is it that some people seem to always be in the right place at the right time while others experience just the opposite? These are nothing more than time-correlated restrictions or their closely related converse, impositions, where serendipity plays a role in our personal development.

Many restrictions are designed into our incarnational plan, prior to birth. Metaphysically, these restrictions are based on the learning to be accomplished in this particular life. As such, in the physical, they are simply the tool used to keep us focused on living out that plan.

Restrictions are not a form of predestination, rather they control the presentation of life's choices so that we have the best opportunity for living a successful life. Success in the metaphysical sense has nothing to do with bank accounts, vacation homes or boats. Rather, it is based on the fulfillment of our particular incarnational life plan.

True spirituality is the living of our life on the basis of who we really are rather than who we think we ought to be. From the metaphysical or nonphysical perspective, true spirituality has nothing to do with any particular religion or metaphysical practice.

The physical body is but a symbol of the nonphysical consciousnesses manifesting it. Thus it is an identity with our spiritual essence. Growth in either domain is reflected by growth in the other, thus the axiom: spiritual growth cannot be, nor ever is, sacrificed by growth in the physical.

And so life on earth is about the experience of self, about living life on our own terms, but only within the relatively narrow scope defined by our particular incarnational restrictions. Growth realized by living through our life learning lessons brings on new insight, and it is this that reveals who we are. Through this experience, life expands our perspective.

Taken together, this is the essential method and principle of spiritual growth using the earth experience. When we in the physical get off track of our incarnational plan, restrictions limit us through an experience called an illness. Healing takes place when we get "back on track" in compliance with our incarnational plan.

Life is intended to be a matter of personal exploration and experiment of self. When life is experienced in this way, it becomes effortless and joyful, gently flowing around you. As this flow proceeds, you experience how life relates to you, rather than how you relate to it or some particular (and exterior) facet of it brought into your life through authority or other figures.

Living life this way is living a spiritual life. It is through the discovery of self while using the metaphor of physical life that we are healed and our restrictions are released.

ENERGY HEALING DEFINED

Rephrased slightly, healing is the release of restrictions that prevents our experience of life on our own terms through an unimpeded self-response to reality. Healing isn't just about recovering from injury or sickness. Rather, it is a form of practical or applied spirituality. Restrictions in any form can and should be looked upon as an illness waiting to be healed. Once the necessary learning and experience have taken place, the illness dissolves as the restriction is lifted, thus allowing further exploration and growth.

Conversely, illness should always be looked upon as a restriction of self-expression, regardless of its manifestation. Restrictions are always related to the fundamentals of the life being led by the individual experiencing them and never about others. Thus, healing is an internal, largely nonphysical process, the result of acquiring experience at some level of consciousness within our physical body.

Healing always brings on a new level of thinking because healing insight introduces new perspective at the consciousness level where the healing took place. As a practice, then, the practice of healing is simply one of applied insight.

We are often not consciously aware of the underlying learning that is taking place, although when completed it is often revealed by such expressions as, "Boy, I'll never try that one again!" or "I'm sure glad that's over." Or perhaps, "I may have learned a lot, but I never want to go through that again!"

In the final analysis, healing changes the reality of the person being healed by increasing perspective. This is an important concept for it broadens the scope of what healing is really about and how it has application in almost every aspect of daily life. As such, healing, by very definition, is spiritual growth, fulfilling creation's fundamental imperative.

CHAPTER 2

NONPHYSICAL HUMAN ANATOMY

Once you can accept the universe as matter expanding into nothing that is something, wearing stripes with plaids comes easy.
—Albert Einstein

Our human nature has both a physical body, the one we use in our normal day-to-day living, and a nonphysical body that surrounds and encases our physical selves. The nonphysical side of us, which nearly anyone with an interest can learn to detect, is "energy-based." There are four easily sensed "energetic" bodies surrounding the physical body, plus several more that typically only sensitives can discern. Energy, as the word is used here, is a nonphysical, energetic principle that usually carries intent that affects the consciousnesses to whom it is directed.

The nonphysical body as viewed by a healer contains seven major energy centers called chakras. These energy centers are located vertically along the physical spinal column and vector energy of a specific type for each chakra. Six "lesser" chakras are located two on the palms of the hands, two very minor chakras on the knees, and two on the feet.

As far as those living in the physical realm are concerned, probably the most commonly held outlook is that we live our lives totally in the physical world. However, there is a strong belief and desire established in most religions that, upon death, we exit into a spiritual or otherwise nonphysical world. Some philosophical views deny both the nonphysical aspects of ourselves and our survival after death.

The metaphysical viewpoint agrees that we live in the physical world, but argues that we simultaneously exist as a spiritual essence in a mirrored nonphysical state as well. Thus the definition of an incarnated spirit becomes one that is temporarily bound to a being in the physical universe. Our essential position is that death simply marks an unbinding of the spirit, freeing it to return to the fully nonphysical state. This results in the de-animation of the body which we call death.

Although the information contained in this and the following chapters is pertinent for all forms of life and consciousnesses, our purpose here is to provide only that level of essential understanding necessary for those wishing to develop their own advanced healing skills and techniques. The discussion of metaphysical aspects concerning consciousness and non-physical energies, both here and elsewhere, is thereby limited but taken up in Chapter 3.

Energy Model of the Human Being

Western knowledge of human energy systems has largely come to us from a single source, that being the book *The Serpent Power* by Arthur Avalon, first published in 1919 in England. This book is a difficult read. Although intended for those practicing yoga, healers should at least be aware of this classic as it serves as the definitive word on the subject of human energy systems as far as the yoga tradition goes. And so it has application in the healer's art.

Our look at the human energy system is strictly from the energy healer's perspective and differs in many respects to that of classical yoga. The healer's art is in manipulating the energy by externally changing its flow, removing unneeded or interfering energy, and introducing new energy into the nonphysical body for the purpose of removing metaphysical restriction which will be discussed shortly. We operate at the physical, the nonphysical, and the mental levels. Those practicing various forms of yoga do so internally, for different reasons and through a totally different philosophy.

The Chakras

Chakras are energy centers that are located throughout the body. The traditional view of them is shown in Drawing 2-1 and consists of seven main chakras located along the spine and head. The healer's perspective is that life (or animation) energy flows from our spiritual essence into the crown chakra at the top of the head. From there it is propagated downward to the root chakra near the anus, passing along the way the chakras of the brow or third eye, the throat, heart, solar plexus, and the sacrum. Energy unused as it travels this course is stored in reserve.

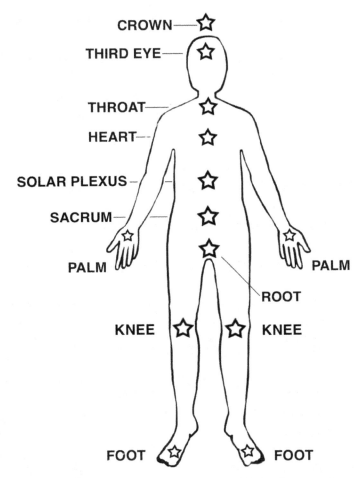

Drawing 2-1 Front view of the physical body showing the most active chakras. The chakras can be detected from the front of the body, but generally not from the back.

The traditional yoga views on energy are established through its study of the kundalini, symbolized as a coiled serpent living in the root chakra. When released, the kundalini travels upward from the root with unpredictable impact on the individual. Speaking from some personal experience, when this happens, it is an event that will not soon be forgotten.

Healers soon discover four additional but smaller chakras useful to their practice. Two are located in the palm of each hand and two more on the soles of the feet, near the pads behind the toes. Depending on the source of your information, the actual number of energy centers in the human being has been put in the thousands, but for energy healing work, the eleven just mentioned are the most significant.

Because chakras are nonphysical in nature, they are co-resident with the physical body, not "in" as a part of it. The chakra system is a part of the collective nonphysical body. From the healer's perspective, the chakras provide the behavioral interface between the physical and nonphysical bodies as they communicate via the energy channel running between them and the life energy link, located above the crown chakra.

Chakras are traditionally symbolized as "lotus blossoms" with differing numbers of petals and colors associated with each, although neither the colors nor form are universal. The lotus blossom symbology sometimes becomes an attractive art form which has little to do with the actual chakras.

Each chakra has a unique sound that some adepts can discern. The Sanskrit names given the chakras are said to be similar in nature to the sound each chakra makes. It is possible to stimulate the chakras with sound, typically with chants. While in a deep meditative posture such stimulation can release the energy held "in the chakra" which brings with it enlightenment at that level of consciousness. Given the proper pitch and focused attention, many body parts can also be stimulated in this way.

Most of the main chakras radiate outward from the front of the body, away from the main energy trunk, but the crown chakra is unique. The receptor for life energy, it points straight up through the top of the head, then feeds energy via the energy conduits to the other chakras. The root chakra points outward, but downward at some angle. Two of the minor chakras, located in each hand, point away from the palms and the two others are in each foot near the pad behind the toes point downward, toward the floor.

With considerable practice and effort, the exact location and radiation

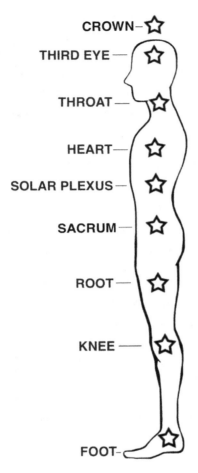

CROWN—

THIRD EYE —

THROAT —

HEART—

SOLAR PLEXUS —

SACRUM —

ROOT —

KNEE —

FOOT—

Drawing 2-2 Viewed from the side, most chakras radiate outwards from the front of the body, with only the root chakra pointing somewhat downward, and the crown straight up. The chakras are indicated as shown for clarity.

angles of the chakras can be reliably discovered by scanning for them as will be described later in Chapter 4. The backs of the chakras connect to a nonphysical energy trunk running vertically along the spine. Within this conductor are said to be many "tubes" that conduct energy of differing types between the chakras for both nourishment and communication.

Although main chakras and this energy conductor are the most active nonphysical features, there are many, many other energy centers and conductors to be found scattered throughout the body. Of primary concern to those practicing acupuncture and moxibustion, through smaller energy centers and related interconnecting energy pathways, they can affect every bodily part and its related sensation to one degree or another.

Energy radiating from the chakras can be easily sensed by most healers during their first day of Reiki 1 training. Advanced healers can sense but also make use of this energy.

ENERGY FLOW BETWEEN THE PHYSICAL AND NONPHYSICAL BODIES

The flow of energy through the main chakras causes combinations of neural stimulants to be constantly and dynamically released from the various bodily glands associated with the individual chakras. This happens as a direct response to the reality sensed by the individual at any given time. Once these chemicals enter the bloodstream and reach the brain, they alter the way it processes information by selectively stimulating or suppressing brain activity at various locations.

Perceptually, this alters the manner in which reality is sensed and reported to our awareness, which then, as a second order effect, alters the way our natural or nonphysical response is expressed back into the physical. Since the early 1990s science has been investigating this general linkage with the discovery of neural stimulants originating in the lower body.

The brain is the center of our awareness, thought processes, and our personality. Being the seat of our physical consciousness, the brain controls the inputs from our five senses to our thought field and physically expresses our personality. Brain-inspired actions are mechanically based on inputs from the five senses, our "mind" and our sense of "self," a memory pattern of many levels, most of them unconscious.

When brain function is altered for any reason, including injury, stimulant or drug use, the perceived reality is also altered because the physical senses are not processed and evaluated in the normal fashion prior to their entry into the thought field. (The thought field is described in Chapter 3.) Under these conditions, our responses may be altered if the injury or chemical intervention is operative at the logical or memory level. Worse, once a response is composed, the impaired brain may alter the flow of the response as an additional function of the impairment.

Thus we can experience a three-stage cascading failure: the senses are skewed, the logical response to them becomes erratic, and the response itself is sometimes altered apart from what it was intended. The result is unpredictable and (possibly) psychotic behavior.

If the impairment to the brain is temporary, such as from alcohol or non-destructive drugs, normal brain function returns once these chemicals are removed from the system, and the personality expression reverts to whatever is normal for that person.

Generally, healers do not deal with those under the influence of such drugs, although it is fairly common to be asked to augment conventional medical treatment that sometimes consists of heavy medication. Care must be exercised when dealing with both the client and caregivers in order to not cause undue expectation or anxiety regarding possible interference. As a rule, the client's incarnational plan and spiritual law will keep the healer from doing accidental harm in these instances. (See Healing Theory and Practice, Chapter 4.)

Free energy flow between the chakras is very important to the individual because without it personality flaws of a wide variety will be manifest. The detection of such blocks is easy, but the clearing of them can range from involved, difficult, or if incarnationally inspired, impossible. This topic is dealt with in some detail in Chapter 4.

THE NONPHYSICAL BODY

We will describe the nonphysical body and its various layers from the inside outward. It is quite difficult to sense more than the innermost four nonphysical layers. When sensed going outward from the physical body, the layers become increasingly ethereal, with the outermost two or three layers usually indiscernible to even the most sensitive healer. Indeed, with over twenty years of experience, I have not discovered the outermost three layers, leading me to question if these layers actually exist. Even so, depending on the source, there are said to be seven or more layers in total.

Although the vast majority of healers (including me) cannot *visually* observe any part of the nonphysical body, most healers, even those just starting their careers, can usually tactilely sense the presence, vitality, and several other conditions of the more physical (inner) layers.

The chakras themselves are usually indicative of energy flow between the various layers and the physical body. With experience, many healers can mentally sense the energy flows but not through normal vision. Rather, the sense of the energy flow is that of flowing colors of energy, as mentally sensed. Energy healers new to the practice can soon learn to sense this flow if properly coached. Any blockage sensed can result in sickness that can introduce profound deleterious effects. Blockages are therefore of more than passing interest.

For the most part, each layer in the nonphysical body is only aware of those layers beneath it, a fairly common trait throughout nature. Our psychological consciousness—the one you are using to read this text—demonstrates this principle. This level of consciousness operates as a part of the physical body. In reality, the physical body is simply the innermost layer of the nonphysical body without any further distinction. This particular aspect of our self-awareness is not generally aware of our nonphysical attributes since by comparison, they are ethereal.

Chakra meditation, if conscientiously practiced, will yield some results, but full realization of what the nonphysical "layers of self" mean cannot be obtained until the nonphysical body associated with a chakra is actually entered by your awareness. It is possible to do this through practiced meditation and much preparation. Each nonphysical layer reveals a particular philosophical perspective or aspect of ourselves.

Exclusively a voyage of self-discovery, this practice and study of self takes more long-term devotion than most living a non-cloistered life are able to give. But it is a dormant opportunity for those healers interested in finding out more about themselves and the world around them. From a purely healer perspective, this subject area is largely diversionary and without special reward.

THE APPEARANCE OF THE NONPHYSICAL BODY

When the nonphysical body is viewed by a sensitive, it is said to first appear as one or more bands of color surrounding the physical body in a halo-like fashion. This is just the fringing around the outer edges of the various nonphysical body layers.

The nonphysical body layers are three-dimensional and completely encase the body. Depending on one's sensitivity, with careful and patient observation, a more complete view of the nonphysical body may eventually emerge. These layers are *not* visible through normal vision, rather, they can be sensed with the eyes closed as patterns of light and color. Developing this visual ability takes time and dedication that most people don't have available.

TABLE 1 - CHARACTERISTICS OF THE MAIN CHAKRAS*

CHAKRA	COLOR	NUMBER OF PETALS	REGANT TATTVA QUALITIES
Crown	Supreme White	1000	
Brow [or third eye]	---	2	Mental Faculties
Throat	White	16	Sense of Hearing
Heart	Smoky	12	Sense of Touch
Solar Plexus	Red	10	Sense of Sight, Color and Form
Abdomen	White	6	Sense of Taste
Root	Yellow	4	Sense of Smell

*Table 2-1*Colors associated with chakras and other nonphysical energy systems are largely subjective and may vary with the healer. These should not be taken as established fact until personally verified. The colors, petal count and senses shown in this chart are taken from The Serpent Power by Arthur Avalon.*

The perceived colors are subtle, to say the least, and whatever is found—if they are found—should not be considered to be "the" color of any one band since colors are dynamic and nearly always changing. This is particularly true of the emotional layer which is in constant turmoil with multiple colors showing most of the time.

THE NONPHYSICAL BODY LAYERS

The Physical Layer is the innermost body layer. It is closely linked with the physical body itself, and in a healthy person typically extends about four to eight inches—and rarely a foot—outside of the body. This layer is quite useful to the healer because it reveals much about what is going on inside the physical body. In purely physical terms, the sensations coming from this nonphysical body are often sensed as heat or coolness on the sensing hand and are fairly easy to discern. This is the field in which we scan for physical problems.

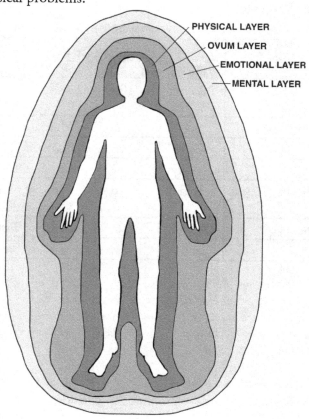

PHYSICAL LAYER
OVUM LAYER
EMOTIONAL LAYER
MENTAL LAYER

Drawing 2-3 This energy model of the body shows the relationship between the physical body and the nonphysical shells surrounding it. Of the shells, the ovum is the most physical, and the mental layer the most ethereal and hardest to discern.

The Ovum Layer is located outside the physical layer. It is called "ovum" because this nonphysical body is the first to abandon the contour of the physical body and become more egg-shaped. The ovum is manifest as a band of energy extending to perhaps a foot from the physical body. It holds most of our reserve metaphysical energy, and so its size is fairly indicative of the client's overall physical state and health. When a person is seriously ill or run-down, this field shrinks. Still fairly physical, with practice it can be easily sensed by most people.

The Emotional Layer is the most complex of the nonphysical layers. Typically extending about eight to twelve inches beyond the ovum, its depth varies greatly from one individual to the next. Associated with the solar plexus chakra, the emotional body is a major gateway from which thought influences the physical body and invokes responses of all kinds. It is highly influenced by virtually every aspect of the life being led. The main processor of our response to reality, this body indicates the energy exchanges passing through the various chakras at any given time.

The Mental Layer is less complicated than the Emotional Layer and typically usually displays two colors to those who can perceive it indicating the two modes of thinking, that of intuitive processing and that of intellect. But as always, these may vary. This layer expands and contracts, becoming more dense when smaller and generally ranges between eight and twelve inches in thickness.

This layer indicates the individual's predominant approach to life, whether intellectual or intuitive. The outside portion of this layer, being closer to external stimuli and less physical, operates the fastest. Thus, it usually defines the mode of thinking and behavior that is strongest but is by no means exclusive. Another function of this body is to coordinate the conscious and unconscious minds. When both minds are synchronized, a state with no internal mental stress is entered, a rare occurrence for most.

The Paraconscious Layer is named in honor of Jack Schwarz, the Dutch metaphysicist of extraordinary gifts who first used this term. (See www.throughyourbody.com/jack-schwarz-mind-matter/) This is the body that carries the incarnational plan and the lessons to be learned. It is the source of our thoughts and conscious awareness of the physical and the seat of our human conscious awareness, creativity, and intuition.

Between twelve and eighteen inches thick, this body is not influenced by the turmoil of day-to-day life. Normally, human conscious awareness does not extend beyond the Paraconscious Layer.

The Causal Layer serves many purposes and could be considered our incarnated spirit or soul because it retains those learning plans that require multiple lifetimes to complete. It is also responsible for processing the pure, white broad spectrum of life energy arriving at the crown chakra into the component and constituent parts that are available for the present incarnation as prescribed by the Paraconscious Layer.

In essence, it filters the broad spectrum life energy that we receive, passing on only that energy that is the basis of this particular incarnation. It is thus the first of several devices used by the incarnational principle to restrict our consciousness. The Causal Layer is the interface between our human consciousness, spiritual essence and the nonphysical realm of unlimited potential and possibility.

The Cosmic, or Spiritual, Layer is where our spiritual essence begins. Very little is knowable about this level of awareness from the human level of consciousness, and so descriptions of it must come from adepts who have spent the majority of their lives in dedicated study.

VIEWING THE NONPHYSICAL BODY LAYERS

At the time of this writing, there were no known physical instruments capable of photographing, measuring or sensing nonphysical human energy systems, chakras, the nonphysical bodies or "auras." It remains to be seen whether or not there is more than a coincidental connection between these purely physical fields and metaphysical energy systems. So far virtually everything published on this subject outside of established scientific journals is purely speculative.

Very few people claiming to "see" the nonphysical bodies have had their vision scientifically appraised. Of those who can (or claim to) authentically visualize nonphysical energy systems at work, most have a greatly expanded range of color vision. When Jack Schwarz was tested at the University of Washington during the early 1970s, it was found that he could see light wavelengths from 335 (above ultraviolet light) to 1700 (below infrared) nanometers.

This is an extraordinary increase—about four times—over normal human color vision acuity which usually ranges from about 400 (violet) to 700 (red) nanometers and shows that he had very special physical vision. But if this were all there was to it, cameras and films easily capable of rendering accurate and scientifically valid photographs of such non-physical energy phenomena would have been developed—and applied—long ago.

In the final analysis, it is not necessary nor particularly advantageous for healers to see the nonphysical layers since they can be felt tactilely. Indeed, such an ability, insofar as the healer is concerned, is more likely to be a diversion than an asset because it may drive a temptation to diagnose from the head, rather than heal from the heart.

Having said that, sicknesses stemming from mental trauma, or being projected as an incarnational issue, start as a nonphysical phenomenon within these bodies. Over the course of about six months, the illness gains physicality as it slowly migrates toward the physical body. These issues can be sensed by most healers while the affliction is still nonphysical. Depending on the circumstances and issues surrounding the illness, the grounding caused by it may be averted or abbreviated if it is intercepted and the issues causing it healed while it is still in the nonphysical state.

It is often the case that the healer can detect an oncoming illness but cannot resolve or diminish its effect. This may be due to incarnational factors or the client's unwillingness to resolve the issues causing it.

LIFE ENERGY FLOW IN THE HUMAN BODY

The life force or animating energy coming into the human body is passed to the crown chakra via the ray channel. The ray channel provides the direct connection to the energy coming from the incarnated spirit. Some say the energy flow itself takes on the form of a spiral or cone, the pointed end terminating within the crown chakra itself. I personally have not seen the ray channel, although it is easily sensed tactilely.

Life energy comes from the spiritual essence that we are, our higher self or higher power as the case may be. Although it starts out as broadband or white energy, components of this energy flow are filtered out as a part of the incarnational plan as previously mentioned. In the physical sense, this is performed in the ray channel as the energy flows into the crown chakra.

If the incoming energy is visualized as "light," then life energy starts out as "white" (composed of all colors) at the top entry point on the ray. The ray represents the quality of the energy passing into the crown, indicating the thinking mode, behavior and life interests of the individual.

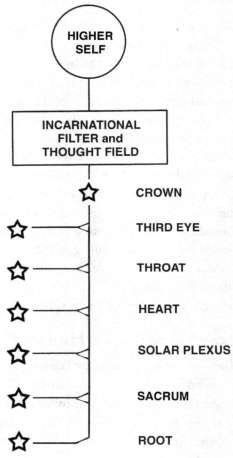

HIGHER SELF

INCARNATIONAL FILTER and THOUGHT FIELD

CROWN

THIRD EYE

THROAT

HEART

SOLAR PLEXUS

SACRUM

ROOT

Drawing 2-4 Full-spectrum energy is provided by our higher power (or higher self). It is filtered by the incarnational model to suit our life learning plan. The focus center is controlled by our five physical senses and by our thought field. Once the energy reaches the thought field, the mind consumes as much as 85% of it before it is passed on to our body.

The energy itself is tailored to the specific needs of the individual throughout his lifetime. Thus, it is subject to change in both intensity and color as the individual progresses and ages. Generally, the energy flowing through the ray channel is too ethereal to be physically sensed, but with meditation and a lot of effort, most healers can eventually obtain a sense of their own energy flow.

The energy that enters the body in the crown chakra ultimately flows past the other various chakras via the transmission conduits running along the spine that were described earlier. This energy is tapped as it passes by each chakra and whatever remains is stored as reserve energy in the root chakra. The life energy flow is continuous and ends only upon death, the result of our spiritual manifestation being withdrawn from the physical.

The reserve energy held in the chakras and nonphysical bodies is the energy that most "natural" healers call upon when they perform a healing. As a result, when giving of this energy, the majority become tired or "run down" after performing extensive or complex healings. Particularly active natural healers often suffer significant health problems of their own because their energy reserves are chronically depleted.

Because the energy is filtered prior to entering the natural healer's body, its healing efficacy and scope are limited by the essential nature of the particular individual healer. This causes most to specialize their healing practice. For example, a natural healer may be able to heal a particular type of animal, such as horses, better than another.

Healing energies such as Reiki and Johrei™ are not stored or storable in significant quantity within the healer's body, although it can certainly be used to heal the healer. The Reiki tradition, in fact, teaches that Reiki healing energy is meant primarily for the healer, next for the healer's circle of family and friends, and only then is it meant to be used to heal the general public.

The inability to store Reiki healing energy within ourselves is a common metaphysical trait. Psychic awareness, for the most part, exists only on demand. Esoteric knowledge behaves the same way, manifesting only when needed or called upon. In other words, Reiki healing energy, psychic information, and esoteric knowledge are only available when needed, and when it is not, they are gone without a trace.

It is an efficient system. The sensitive is never cluttered with information not germane to the present moment. It takes an uncommonly high level of self-trust to perform under these conditions because going into a session, the healer or sensitive hasn't a clue or thought about what will be discovered or what should be done. Trust in self allows one to go into harm's way, knowing full well that what is needed will always be provided. But only when that right time comes along.

ENERGY FLOW PROCESSING WITHIN THE BODY

Before the life energy is accessible to us in the physical, it passes through the incarnational constrictions and filters previously mentioned as being located in the ray channel. It must be emphasized that although the nature of a few of these filters and the general mechanisms of the process have been identified, they are all under incarnational control and subject to variation from individual to individual.

As such, there is no way for us to tamper with or adjust these devices. Incarnational features will not significantly change unless the individual accomplishes all the learning outlined by the plan. Nor, in my opinion, is tweaking various incarnationally inspired conditions likely to ever be possible from our physical perspective. It is not our purpose in life to second-guess our reason for being here, however hurtful that realization may seem to our tender egos.

Without the perspective engendered by knowing a part of the plan, there is little to be gained and everything to lose by fiddling with something we know nothing about. Yet there are those of us with a curiosity about it all. If the incarnational philosophy described thus far had no role to play in the healer's growth or validation, then we would have no interest, ability, or talent to explore this area of self.

Whatever your view on this subject, we now complete our survey of our nonphysical structure with a look at the logical flow of energy within our body as we attempt to classify the several operations performed on life energy before it can be utilized as a part of our personal manifestation and life's work. This will give another view of the same mechanisms at work. It is up to you, the reader, to allow these views to combine into a cohesive understanding of the principle.

36

Life energy (including healing energies such as Reiki) is provided to our manifestation via the spiritual essence that we, as individuals, are. There are many terms for this concept, among them god, deity, higher power, and higher self. The distinction between these terms is described in Chapter 3, The Higher Self, but for this discussion, we simply assert that this principle, by whatever name, is the source of our nonphysical energy and represents our connection to the nonphysical realm.

From the logical perspective, energy first enters our body system through the crown chakra which supplies some of the filtering function described earlier as taking place in the ray.

The incarnational filter is a tool that encodes the learning lessons to be accomplished in this lifetime, regulating and restricting the flow of energy to that which is appropriate for this particular life. It is also through this "filtering" mechanism that we lose awareness of our true spiritual essence. Thus, we are aware only of the limited set of talents and abilities that our rational mind assumes is all that we are.

Energy leaving the incarnational filter flows down the energy channels, into and out of the chakras as already described. This energy is available to the entire system upon demand, although its effects are primarily limited to internal mental effects, such as driving self-trust, motivation, and sustaining external interests.

Another way of expressing this concept is to view who we really are as a subset of our total spiritual essence. This is symbolized by the animation energy entering our nonphysical body structure. Because of the linkage between our physical and nonphysical bodies, and the genetic coding imposed along with other development of the body in its embryonic and fetal stages, the physical body is the physical manifestation of the incarnational plan. As a group, the nonphysical layers define not only our personality, but also our creativity and potential, and are representative of our present state of incarnational development.

The importance of this concept cannot be over-emphasized. Without the input of the animation energy, there would be no energy for our human awareness to function, let alone for our body to operate as it should. Overall, this is the system that keeps us alive and on track throughout our lives.

As a mechanism of selective energy management, the incarnational system provides an integrated means for controlling the amount and types of energy supplied to the body. These are physically manifest by the release of neural stimulants in the body that ultimately control brain function. As such, it provides the means for denying energy in the form of talent, ability, and even interest in those areas or fields of endeavor that are not relevant or are destructive to a particular incarnational life plan.

The physical body plays a key role in a complex system of focused awareness and learning. If a physical life is to be lived in a particular way as defined by the incarnational plan, then it is vitally important that the body be able to support those aspects essential for the life to be experienced. The physical attributes of the body are the final set of restrictions needed to set an incarnational plan into motion.

THE MIND

Before the energy leaving the incarnational filter can be used, it is tapped by the mind. The mind is a brain function that consumes lots of energy, perhaps as much as 85% of the incoming energy in adults. It does not return that energy or exchange it; it consumes it. The mind itself is the seat of all logic, one based on the comparison of two entities or objects. In practice, its primary products are our view of reality as seen through our five senses and its various defensive postures.

Anatomically, the mind interfaces to the main energy trunk as a part of the incarnational filter and the energy conduits feeding the rest of the system. It therefore has access to virtually all of the energy flowing into the body.

The rational mind, which started to appear in significant numbers in the human population roughly 4,500 years ago, has changed, if not pirated, a good deal of the earth experience. Its original purpose was to generate alternative choices of action based on the reality being reported by the five senses at any given time. The actual result has been an unexpected integration into our self-awareness as a part of rational thought.

That the mind is a good and useful tool cannot be denied. It works tirelessly, at peak producing three or four (and perhaps more) alternative courses of action each second. A sort of internal "brainstorming" center, this is a good thing when you need to solve problems. The mind can be trained for use in any occupation, solving problems from survival in harsh desert or arctic environments where mere survival is an accomplishment, to designing rockets and spacecraft. It is a versatile, multifaceted tool.

Unfortunately, three features of the mind make it a real problem for most people. First and perhaps foremost, it doesn't have an identity linkage that ties it to you, and so your awareness is surrounded—obscured is not too strong a word—by it. The mind is purely mechanical in its approach and thus treats you as just another object to be manipulated, compared and ultimately discarded. It has no friends, and left to its own, builds and maintains enormous defensive structures when it feels threatened, which is the majority of the time. Its primal goal is to avoid pain and to maximize pleasure, which it does by instilling various defensive behaviors. Although the defenses are really for it and not for you, the resulting behavior it imposes is seen from the outside as who you apparently are.

The second feature is that the mind normally has free reign to blather about anything and everything being experienced. Its strong point is comparison against a reference, and so it uses whatever it encounters at the moment as the reference point for judgment of everything and everybody, including yourself. As a part of this, it usually accepts other people as authorities to be aspired to, thus demeaning your self-image through trivialization. Such mental sludge ordinarily covers and mutes many if not most of our natural responses to self.

And finally, the mind uses the results of its calculations, however atrocious or inappropriate, as fact to base new "opportunities" on the basis of that flawed logic. It is incapable of recognizing that it is in error or that it can make a mistake. Given that the mind is the basis for all logic, at any one time, it always makes sense to you, even when it is outrageously wrong in the eyes of those around you. And it will stand by its conclusions, building defense upon defense until the cows come home.

Eventually, usually by the time we reach our late twenties, it is consuming 70% or more of our energy purely for self-justification and maintenance of its defensive postures. Each of us pays the price for this wasted energy and false images being projected on our behalf. This leaves us with reduced energy to pursue life on our own terms, and so we live with crippling self-criticism and fear.

Although it might seem that the mind is all powerful, particularly since it has access to so much of our energy, this isn't actually the case. The amount of energy it is allowed to consume is based entirely on our willingness to grant it that energy. Although powerful indeed, it can still be controlled by us if we take the initiative.

From the healer's perspective, the mind is of little use and can be quite detrimental since we are not in the business of diagnosing ailments, selecting remedies or speculating on the causes of illness. Our healing art depends entirely on our intuitive talents and abilities. Logic and rationalization, in our case, can only lead to defensive behavior that inhibits our willingness to express ourselves as the healers we are. Thus rational thought, or any input from the mind, prevents us from doing our best work because it can only blur and desensitize our focus on the knowledge of our heart.

We as healers can make the most effective use of the mind by turning it completely off when it is not needed, using it only when problem-solving or a planning issue is at hand. Unfortunately, this is far easier said than done and without specific training, this is a practical impossibility for most people. Traditionally it is resolved by meditation leading to "living in the moment," but the devotion to this project is beyond the practical means of most people and not a subject covered in this book.

The Energy Channels and Ray

Several pathways leading through the nonphysical bodies provide a means for receiving, exchanging or moving energy as well as expelling energy from our energy systems. These channels are located around the crown chakra and are used when the energy being manipulated is not to be changed or damaged. They are not visible and are usually closed, but can be visualized tactilely by the sensitive.

I am not able to sense the colors of the nonphysical bodies or of other nonphysical energy systems. Indeed, I cannot sense many of the "components" of the nonphysical bodies often described in the popular press, leading me to question whether such structures and colors actually exist.

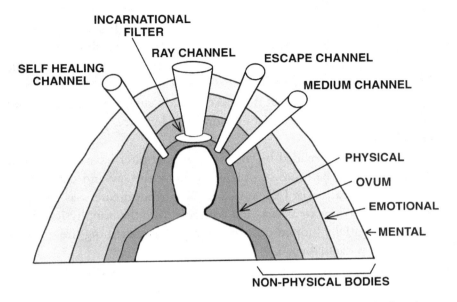

Drawing 2-5 Among others, four general types of key channels can be found going into the crown chakra. Most prevalent is the single ray, shown in the center, but it is not uncommon for two or more other channels to be present. The general behavior of people seems in some ways related to the ray cone size. The various channels shown are located around the top of the head (among others not shown). These are shown in no particular pattern and are for reference only.

As shown in Drawing 2-5, the main source of life energy comes through the connection to the nonphysical via the ray (or other channels). Once again, the energy entering through this channel is of broad spectrum and supplied by who you are as a spiritual essence. The escape channel allows you to expel energy (such as attached spirits) without damage. The self-healing channel allows healing energy from your personal reserve energy to be sent out. And the medium channel provides a safe way to communicate with spirits. Not shown is the Reiki channel among others. The positions shown for the various channels and their construction varies and is for reference only.

THE THIRD EYE

The third eye is actually a part of the focus center. It is used primarily for spiritual communication, clairvoyance, remote viewing, and other nonphysical processes that manifest directly into human awareness. This channel is open to whatever extent it is as a matter of the incarnational plan and the present state of the individual. In many, if not most, cases it is closed, opening only under extraordinary instances that deeply affect the individual.

The functions provided by the incarnational filter have already been described, but to be more complete, we show the ray and channels in their general location in Drawing 2-5. We further define it as that area from which we draw new ideas and concepts from the nonphysical. Such ideas are essentially limited only by the experience defining the spiritual essence that we actually are.

However, the incarnational filter also limits and translates incoming raw energy into incarnationally appropriate energies as a source of our incarnational limitations. Along with these limitations, our creativity is also limited, generally to only that arena provided by our physical reality.

THE MEDIUM CHANNEL

The medium channel is located on the top of the head typically off to one side. If it is open (and operable) as a matter of the incarnational plan, external energy in the form of disincarnate spirits can temporarily enter this channel and communicate through the medium. Usually, the communication is performed verbally or through handwriting, but other body language, such as dance and gesture, is not rare, particularly in Eastern cultures.

The medium channel is most often used when channeling spirits of the deceased, but it can be used for personal purposes as well, such as communicating with one's higher self or power, and other spirits with whom the medium has developed a relationship. It should be noted that the longer a "channeled" spirit has been dead, the more general and incoherent its speech becomes. This is because the spirit is slowly leaving behind the physical, and this includes memory as a decaying artifact of its once physical life.

The channel has two states, that of being open and of being closed. Once the channel is open, it is simply a matter for the medium to invite the intended spirit to enter through it and then be willing to temporarily abandon personal use of the voice or hand control. There is usually no doubt when a spirit has entered the channel.

Ideally, the medium channel is only opened when there is a desire or reason to communicate to a particular spiritual essence, but this is not always the case. Those with unrecognized medium abilities and a freely open medium channel have frequent vivid dreams, disturbed and restless sleep and often complain of a general malaise. Less common in adults, many younger mediums describe hearing voices or having "hidden friends" inside their heads, particularly in childhood.

It is not uncommon for a spirit to get comfortable and "camp out" in such a person for extended periods of time, eventually becoming a real pest. This is a frequent occurrence with young mediums who, while still in grade school, spend a lot of time with a Ouija™ board and other "psychic" tools.

When this happens, the effects are usually similar to a very gentle spiritual possession. However, it is not a case of full-blown possession which should be avoided at all costs. With just a little guidance and experience younger mediums learn to voluntarily eject the spirit and prevent its re-entry by keeping the channel closed. There is little danger to the medium going through these experiences for there is incarnational protection built into their lives. But still, learning to control one's mediumship can be a trying period for both parent and child.

Learning to use the medium channel and to automatically keep it closed when such communication is not desired is problematic for some people. Those with open medium channels attract spirits like magnets, and are often plagued at night by spirits trying to "get through." True mediumship can only come to those who exhibit great self-trust as evidenced by their well developed lower three chakras. For them, mediumship is a natural and incarnationally protected activity.

THE ESCAPE CHANNEL

The escape channel is provided as a way to eject or expel internal energy back into the nonphysical without damaging or altering its constitution. This can be energy that is no longer needed or desired, a projection of a request of some kind, or an attached spirit. This is a "one-way" channel, and normally outside energy cannot enter through it.

This channel safely and usually quite quickly conveys energy through the nonphysical bodies and into the nonphysical realm without change or damage. Another of its most common uses is for ejecting attached spirit consciousnesses. In popular language, this action is called a spiritual exorcism. But as practiced by the advanced healer, this action has nothing in common with the confrontational approaches used in religious exorcisms.

THE SELF-HEALING CHANNEL

The self-healing channel allows healing energy to be directed toward a client. It transmits energy from your personal supply rather than like Reiki which is separate in purpose and does not use personal energy. Use of the self-healing channel does not require Reiki initiation or training as it is a natural feature in every human to one degree or another. The healing technique used with this channel is to send healing energy through it and to drain the residue and healing artifacts through the escape channel or via the hand or foot chakras.

Natural healers make extensive but usually unconscious, use of this channel, and because it uses their personal energy, healing others can become a tiring process that limits their ultimate capability. However, many natural healers are very powerful and have tremendous ability, clearly showing that their incarnational plan provided significant reserve energy to use for this purpose.

THE REIKI ATTUNEMENT CHANNEL

The last nonphysical feature of the human anatomy that we'll discuss is the Reiki (or other) attunement channel, not shown in drawing 2-5. In most people, including natural healers, this channel is available, but until

USING THE SELF-HEALING CHANNEL

Significantly, the best use of this channel involves the removal of old or damaged energy as the new energy is introduced to the body, and so technically, it is an empathic healing approach.

Start your use of this healing technique with the following protocol, adjusting it to suit your needs after you've become familiar with its use:

1. Establish an increased inward flow of energy from the crown chakra by draining as described later in Draining Exercises.
2. Keep the crown chakra open to maintain its inward energy flow.
3. Relax the crown chakra to include the self-healing channel. This intent opens the channel and makes its energy—which is specifically tailored for healing—available to whom or whatever you are healing.
4. Open the escape channel. Through intent, allow the old, spent energy associated with those areas being healed to propagate to the escape channel where it is expelled.
5. Continue for as long as you wish, understanding that the healing achieved with this technique will probably require rest to restore your reserve energy used by the process. If desired, you can use Reiki in conjunction with the energy coming in from the crown channel. This process is one that you'll want to experiment with to find the protocol that works best for you.
6. Close natural healing and the escape channels.

specifically opened, it lies dormant. The usual reason for it being closed is due either to incarnational issues stipulating that it not be available at all, or that its use is not currently appropriate for the individual because of any particular reason. For all others, being able to use Reiki is at least a possibility.

Although the traditional view holds that everyone has the ability to perform Reiki, this is not true. A more correct way of expressing this apparent condition is that "everyone with an interest in the practice of healing has the ability to perform Reiki." Those without the ability typically have no interest, making the original premise self-fulfilling.

It is important to understand that nothing is actually "added" to the human system by Reiki attunements. The healing attunement process, which varies from culture to culture around the world, is actually a spiritual awakening, the on-demand opening of a door that enables healing energy to flow through the crown chakra and into the energy system of the initiate. The change appears to be irreversible. Once this door is opened, I have no experience in which it was possible—or desirable—to close it.

In the context of this chapter, the attunement process opens a previously unused energy channel to the crown chakra. Like the medium channel, it is under conscious control of the healer, although there are times when the energy flows for no apparent reason.

By way of example, similar but different techniques are used by Tibetan monks who practice Tummo. This technique releases a warming energy stemming from the root chakra which causes a heat flash throughout the body. Others have developed means of releasing kundalini energy, which, like Tummo, is energy that propagates from the lower chakras upward through the main energy conduit.

Energies such as these, when transferred from the lower chakras at the levels demonstrated by various monks, are powerful and forceful. If not handled properly it can be dangerous in both the mental and physical domain. Happily, finding these abilities takes years of study and practice which enables the monks to learn how to safely handle these forces.

The main energy principle manifest through the use of Reiki is that of insight. Perspective, reinforcement, and support can be derived from insight as secondary effects when necessary. Reiki energy passes through the crown chakra and the incarnational filter unchanged in function but controlled to exclude incarnationally inappropriate energy and inappropriate or dangerous energy levels. This makes it safe for the healer and recipient alike.

Finally, Reiki or healing energy can always be focused and transformed to fit virtually any need of the healer or recipient. No special meditative methodology is required to augment the practice, although its application and strength continues to improve with consistent usage and experience.

Reiki 1 healers use physical contact as the means of narrowing focus and concentrating intent. Healers with Reiki 2 training can send energy without physical contact provided sufficient focus is maintained. Most healers have not been trained in this technique. Healing by touch continues to be used as the mainstay of most Reiki energy healing practices.

Physical contact is not, and never has been, an essential requirement for projecting energy within the reality space of the healer, although in many cases it is appropriate and psychologically helpful—if not essential—for those receiving it. Human touch is at once comforting and healing within its own right.

When focus is sharply maintained and coupled with intent, Reiki 2 healing energy may be transferred by a simple glance, by blowing it out with the breath, by voice, or by a gesture. The sharper and more defined the healer's focus, the more intense the energy transferred to the receiver will be.

As a general suggestion for those wishing to explore the nonphysical nature of themselves, it will be helpful to change your perspective and thinking that the physical life on the earth is the "default" or normal condition of existence. In fact, it isn't, and there is no real evidence to suggest that this is so. Your awareness, manifesting as it does from the nonphysical, is the only thing that brings the physical world to your attention within the framework of the brain.

Start your understanding at the concept level by thinking of the physical realm as only a temporary condition, and that the nonphysical is by its very nature, the "normal" condition. As such, it is then only a matter of expanding your awareness to discover many of the delights of pure consciousness and through that, the knowledge of the heart.

None of today's scientific equipment has so far been able to measure what we healers call "energy" or "energy flow" in the human body. Yet most interested people, even skeptics, can be taught to successfully and independently witness these phenomena in just an hour or two. I teach this practice as a part of my Reiki 1 class curriculum.

Science has a problem with "subjective observation," such as measurements supported only by the words of those doing the measuring. This is obviously for good reason since much of science depends on precise physical measurement and reproducibility. Anything less just isn't "science."

And so when it comes to measuring and detecting the metaphysical energy systems in the human body, science is at a loss. There is no instrumentation capable of measuring these systems, and even human sensitivities are not reproducible since they vary with the moods of both the person being examined and the examiner.

Compounding the issue, the sensations and visualizations felt by examiners are subjective, with no two examiners always reporting similar—let alone exactly—the same sensations. It is no small wonder that science is skeptical about the entire field of alternative medicine in general and energy healing in particular.

But the acknowledged fact that detection and manipulation of human energy systems are subjective and often variable does not mean that the phenomenon isn't there. Human energy use by cultures have been described and in continuous use since the Egyptian era, and it seems unlikely that this body of knowledge would not have survived the test of time if it held no value.

DISCOVERING THE NONPHYSICAL BODIES

Sensing nonphysical bodies as a presence is done by nearly everyone when some nearby person "feels" too close. As a sensation, it is distinctive but difficult to describe or label. To the non-adept, it feels like an invisible extension to our bodies. It is this sensation that makes a bus or subway feel crowded even when no one is actually bumping into you. It is the feeling you get when someone quietly approaches you from behind, and you can sense it, or the claustrophobic sensation that you feel in cramped quarters even when blindfolded prior to being led into them.

It is possible to control this extension of self. Those involved with entertainment, the stage and performing arts learn this as projection since it allows them to engage the audience, causing it to focus its attention on their performance.

Healers and counselors, on the other hand, find it helpful to pull in their presence so to invite and allow more intimate contact with those who are fearful in their presence. This is the primary tool of empathic healers as well. Powerful healers who fail to notice the space they are occupying in a clinic setting may actually interfere with adjacent healers, causing everything from dizziness to nausea to spontaneous fainting on the part of other healers.

Energy centers and the more physical of the nonphysical bodies are easily found. You'll need not more than an open mind, a willingness to try, and a client volunteer to practice on. If you can't find a human friend, you can start with your family pets—they have, at a lower level, the same sort of energy systems working in their bodies as we do but they are smaller and less easily found unless you have prior experience. The chances are that you can find one in your own body are slim because it is a lot like trying to tickle yourself. For that reason it is best to start this adventure with a volunteer:

Step 1. Begin by asking your volunteer to lie down facing upward on a massage therapy table, couch or on the floor. Situating yourself comfortably to one side, freshen the nerves in your non-dominant hand (many people find it to be the most sensitive for this purpose) by lightly brushing it on your shirt a couple of times.

After doing this notice everything about how your hand feels. It will have a lot of sensations running through it, everything from nearly imperceptible tingles to tickles to small achy feelings, to heat or cold, either singly or all at once. Just witness and quietly observe these sensations as they slowly die down to some steady level. This level is the baseline sensation background that you will learn to sense. It is from this baseline that you will find changes in some way when your hand crosses a chakra or other energy center.

The reason we go through this step is so you can learn the neutral sensations or feelings that constantly come from your hand. Repeat this step several times so that you are aware of how your hand feels when it is detecting nothing but the air around it.

Step 2. Search for an energy center on your volunteer. Of the seven traditional chakras the heart and solar plexus are often the strongest, and so we'll start there.

Freshen your hand once again and wait for the baseline sensations to become apparent. With the thumb and fingers closed together, move your hand horizontally right and left two to six inches above the chest-heart or solar plexus area of your volunteer so that it goes completely across the body side to side. While doing this keep your entire focus on the palm of your hand, maintaining an awareness but no thought about the sensations it is reporting to you. Thought comes from the mind, and it will try to tell you that you can't do it, it is stupid, or why bother.

This is not easy at first. Maintaining an action with only awareness as a guide is not the way most of us operate. When you must think, continuously ask yourself, "What am I feeling in my hand?, What am I feeling in my hand?, What am I feeling in my hand?" You should not allow any other thought than this. But it is still best if you can quiet your mind, so there's no thought at all while you're working.

As you look for the chakra, keep your hand in motion, moving it fairly rapidly across the area you are sensing. It may seem like this should be done slowly so as not to miss the phenomenon. In fact, it is more likely that you'll miss it when you move too slowly. A rapid change in sensation is far easier to detect than a slow one. As you sweep your hand across the heart area, you'll witness a neutral or no sensation period with a rapid rise and fall of sensation as your hand passes over the chakra.

It is important to not anticipate what the sensation will be, nor, after you have discovered a sensation, to think about what it feels like. Don't think about what you're doing—simply witness the sensations on your hand without thought as much as possible, and nothing more.

Chances are excellent that you'll be able to notice a change in the sensations in your hand as it crosses over the center of the body. What does it feel like? It may feel like a small pressure, or a thickening of the air, or as a warmth or heat. Or a coolness. It is a subtle physical sensation, but after you understand what it is that you are looking for, it is unmistakable.

The sensation that you'll feel is applicable only to you and is the way that you'll sense just about all nonphysical energy. Others may pick it up in other ways, but keep in mind that their sense of it is just as valid as yours.

Step 3. Sense the other chakras as well. The root chakra is located at the base of the spine (in the crotch area.) It will be stronger in people with a lot of self-confidence and drive.

The crown chakra faces straight out the top of the head, and so you should orient your palm so that it faces the top of the head. The crown chakra is normally the weakest of the chakras and may extend less than an inch from the scalp. Although you might have trouble finding it, rest assured, everyone has a crown chakra. It is generally most easily detected in people who are more spiritually developed than the general population. The rest of the traditional chakras point straight out the front of the body (except for the root chakra that leaves the body at an angle), and so you will detect them the same way as the heart chakra was found.

Although I don't recommend it, you can also detect energy centers or chakras by use of a pendulum. If you are inclined to do so, try holding a small pendulum over the heart chakra and watch its response.

When the pendulum is in place over an energy field its random wanderings will stop, and it will swing left to right, in and out, or circle in one direction or another. The amplitude of the motion indicates the relative "strength" of the energy source. If it stops moving, it means either that you are a very steady holder or it isn't detecting anything.

When dealing with pendulums, be careful not to drop them on your client. Eye injury is always a present danger when using them around the head. I generally discourage use of pendulums and other dowsing techniques when dealing with human energy systems as being unnecessary crutches, impractical, and potentially dangerous to the subject.

Sensing the Nonphysical Bodies

Once you've learned to reliably detect chakras, you can start learning how to sense the various layers making up our nonphysical bodies. These layers are more ethereal and considerably more subtle than the chakras. The ovum and physical layers, being closest to the physical body, are denser and most have no trouble eventually learning to sense these. Don't perform any of these exercises with the expectation of unfettered success on the first try! It takes practice and persistence.

Step 1. Freshen your sensing hand by lightly brushing it on your shirt, then raise it with the palm facing down as high as you can reach over the shoulder area above your volunteer, who should be lying down and facing up.

Step 2. Focus on the palm of your sensing hand to evoke the intent to sense the nonphysical layers. This is crucial. Metaphysical energy is sensed only on the basis of what your intention is to sense. Once your intent is firmly established, move your hand straight down toward the shoulders of your volunteer. You will eventually be able to feel a thickening or other sensation at several points as your hand approaches the physical body.

If you feel a sensation on the way down, immediately raise your hand back up, observing your hand as the sensation leaves. Bring your hand down to find it again. This is the edge of one of the nonphysical layers. Short term their locations are stable, so if you want to measure its height above the table, you'll find that you hit it within an inch or so just about every time, provided you do it during the same location and session. They vary somewhat on a day-to-day basis. If you compare your results with a friend, you'll probably notice a difference which is based on your sensitivities. Absolute measurements aren't particularly important.

Step 3. Move through it and see if you can find the next lower one. Generally, you will nearly always be able to find the last one, the physical layer, at about six to eight inches above your volunteer. Once you have experience with this technique, you can move your hand through the nonphysical bodies and sense them, one after another.

Step 4. Move to your volunteer's head and see if you can find the very top of the nonphysical body. This is the so-called transpersonal point, as described by W. Brugh Joy's book, *Joy's Way*. Generally, the transpersonal point is quite difficult to find for most people just learning to sense human energy systems.

Start by freshening your sensing hand, then place its back near the top of your volunteer's head, palm facing away. With all of your focus on both the palm and back of your hand, notice the different sensations coming from the palm and the back of your hand. Once you recognize these differences, start moving it away from your volunteer at a slow but steady rate, keeping your focus on both sides of your hand. At some point, typically in the twelve to twenty-four-inch range, this difference vanishes. The transpersonal point varies broadly from person to person, with some extending as much as three to four feet from the top of the head, and others as little as a few inches.

DRAINING EXERCISES

As an exercise, I teach draining at all levels of Reiki as a means of introducing empathic healing techniques. It is a simple way of learning to move energy either in or out of the body. This exercise teaches the technique primarily as a means to remove stress from the body, but it has much broader implications than a simple relaxation tool. It can be performed both at home and in the office but is NOT recommended for use while driving or operating machinery because of the relaxation it causes.

Step 1. Sit in a comfortable chair with your feet flat on the floor and where you can place your hands on something solid. It would be best if you remove your shoes, but this is optional. When you are ready, gently close your eyes and go to Step 2.

Step 2. Place your focus on the bottoms of your feet, and notice for a short time the sensations you feel in them. These are your baseline sensations, similar to those used in your hands that you'll be using shortly. Gently, ever so gently, open the two chakras on the bottom of your feet. Do this by simply relaxing the bottoms of your feet with the intent that the chakras open up so that tired energy can be drained through them. Once you are satisfied that the chakras are open (you feel a change in sensation in your feet), do the same with your hand chakras.

Step 3. Move your focus to your crown chakra and open it to allow fresh energy to start flowing down toward the other chakras, rinsing, filling and flushing each as the energy reaches it. Follow the flushing energy as it flows down your arms and legs and back into the earth where it will be recycled. Allow the flushing period to continue for as long as you wish, maybe another two or three minutes.

Step 4. Place your focus on your root chakra. Open it by relaxing it as before, then allow all the old, tired, stale energy in it to drain out of it and flow down your legs, past the knees, into your feet and down into the earth where it will be recycled. Follow the flow and witness, but don't think about, the sensations as it goes down. Don't worry about the process or an apparent lack of it. Going forward, the observation of sensation and your intent assures that the process is only a matter of practice on your part.

Step 5. Focus on the sacrum (abdominal) chakra and start draining it. Again, follow its flow down to the root chakra where it joins the energy draining from it, then on down to your feet. Repeat this process for the solar plexus chakra.

Step 6. Move your focus to the palms of your hands which should now be resting on something solid beside you, perhaps part of the chair you are sitting on or a table in front of you. Open the chakras on the palms of your hands and as with your feet, witness their baseline sensations as you open your heart chakra. Let the old energy start flowing out of it. Some of it goes down towards the other chakras joining the flow to your feet, and some of it goes down your arms, to your hands, and into the arm of the chair.

Step 7. Open your throat and brow chakras and allow their stale energy to flow down and out your arms and feet as with the heart.

Step 8. Allow the chakras to continue their flow for a couple of minutes. During this time your only job is to witness the flow out of your body. Do not think about or participate in the process in any way.

Step 9. Close off the outgoing flow of energy from each chakra in turn, starting with the brow chakra, (including your hand chakras) finishing with the feet. Allow the chakras to be completely filled with fresh energy from the crown chakra without rushing or worry for another two or three minutes. Allow the crown chakra to close on its own accord. Finally, allow yourself a few minutes to come back to the world, now relaxed, refreshed and rejuvenated.

DRAWING THINGS TO YOU

This exercise teaches—and requires—that you learn to sense your gut feelings. This is an important part of the healer's toolkit. These feelings are reported to you as subtle but quite physical sensations in your stomach and lower abdominal area.

Gut feelings can only tell you one of three things: a positive feeling for yes, meaning that what you see in front of you resonates with you and that you can or should go for it. A negative feeling says that the choice or condition you are looking at has nothing to do with who you are and so it would be best to ignore or stay away from it. The last feeling (or perhaps no feeling at all) is the proverbial shrug of the shoulders that means it doesn't matter what you do so go for it if you like.

You can use your gut feelings along with energy from your root chakra to attract and pull things into you. Alternatively, you can use a pendulum for sensing the body's responses if you like, but it is important as a growing healer that you learn to sense and trust your gut feelings and dispense with unnecessary and encumbering tools of the occult.

When you are ready, do the following steps, but realize they are actually just guidelines. After you've used it several times, consider modifying the process to suit your way of doing things.

Step 1. Drain before starting. While optional, it is best. After draining, with a pencil (or pen) and paper, write down exactly what you want to bring into your life. This step brings your request into the physical so your body can tell you if it is appropriate and cannot be ignored.

If you have trouble phrasing the request, it is your body telling you that there is something wrong with it. When this happens, it is a good opportunity to talk to your body by speaking out loud. Tell it about the problem you want to solve and ask what you should be asking for instead, then write down the insights—not your thoughts—as they flow in. Insights appear as complete patterns that form instantly. Thoughts are always sequentially structured and take time to finish. Ignore thought, it is only input from your mind and cannot be trusted.

Step 2. Place your focus on your stomach and lower abdomen area so that you can sense what your body is telling you about the request you make and be prepared to accept the answer. If the answer is a yes, continue to Step 3. If your answer is a no, your body is telling you to either change the request or give it up. If you decide to attempt to bring your request in through other means, forcing it into your life, then you must be prepared to live with the consequences.

Step 3. Open your root chakra and allow the energy of your request to flow in and mix with it. Maintain your focus on your written request and allow this process to build. The sensations you feel will vary, everything from unsettled bowels to genuine excitement.

Step 4. Place your focus on the top of your head with the intent that it be over your escape channel. Relax the escape channel with the intent that it should open.

Step 5. Allow the excitement energy to flow upwards from your root chakra to the escape channel, watching it without thought as it leaves. As it flows upward, it is not uncommon to feel a rush of heat, particularly if you are new to this technique. This is caused by lack of specific and tightly controlled focus, and the result is that you're also bringing up a lot of extra, unrelated energy. In extreme cases, this can cause dizziness and hot flashes for a brief period. After your request is gone, without thought and by intent alone, close your escape channel and root chakra.

Natural Healing

You can heal yourself and others using your own personal energy. This self-healing exercise is useful even for those with Reiki training as it will teach you more about your own internal energy flow and the communication between the physical and nonphysical body. Steps one and two are significant because the process they reveal demonstrates an alternative approach for obtaining permission to heal. In this case, we are using the nonphysical body to communicate the issues directly to the physical body consciousness by way of written communication.

By this simple demonstration, our entire physical and nonphysical being is asked to negotiate, then exercise a healing. Notice that the healing energy employed in steps one through four is coming from the crown chakra alone. If you desire further, more specific healing, use of the self-healing channel in the crown chakra is described starting at Step 5.

The energy causing the affliction can be flushed out through the feet and drained into the earth, but as Steps 5–6 illustrate, it can also be expelled through the escape channel. As we have no need or desire to keep the energy from the illness intact, it is probably simpler to just flush it through the feet rather than send it back up to the escape channel. It is your choice. Use your own personal experimentation and experience to find which way works best for you.

The healing does not take place until the residual affliction energy leaves the body. This energy is not released by the consciousnesses involved until there is an agreement to be healed, generally a function of learning at some level being completed or a turn towards that learning.

Healing is actuated by insight, and sometimes reinforcement energy being fed from the crown chakra and self-healing channel to the afflicted area. When there is sufficient intent, the driving force behind the healing, and the timing is incarnationally appropriate, an agreement is reached, and a sensitive person can often feel or sense the release of the ailment energy as it takes place. It is at this time that the healing becomes a reality.

The following exercise demonstrates a sophisticated and fully conscious method for obtaining permission to heal. As with a conventional Reiki treatment, permission is always required to heal, even ourselves. This aspect of the healing protocol cannot be ignored if best results are to be obtained regardless of the healing methodology used.

Step 1. Start the draining exercise described previously, but do not close off the flow from the chakras—just let them continue to flush. Once this is accomplished, with pencil and paper, make your request physical by writing it down. If you find difficulty in writing or phrasing the request, it indicates an unwillingness to be healed at some level. If this happens, explore what the problem is and physically write whatever insights come to mind.

You may end up having to request healing insight to enable the healing to proceed later, rather than a direct healing. Don't do this on a computer—it must be done by hand with pencil (or pen) and paper. This is to make the request more "physical."

Step 2. Ask yourself the following questions by writing them out as you continue to drain. Of course, you can add to the list, but don't do this as a planned ritual. Candles and incense will not help the process. Simply write out the questions, then jot down the answers and insights—but not your thoughts—as they pop into mind. Valid answers and insights will appear on their own as a complete thought all at once in a flash. They do not include a "preamble" or a "chain of thought" leading to a conclusion. All that is necessary is for you to quiet your mind (try not to think) while writing out the answers to the following questions:

1) Am I willing to deal with the fundamental cause of the affliction that I wish to heal?
2) Am I ready to release my desire for the sympathy this affliction brings me?

As an experiment, you could also try using a pendulum to register the responses, but the results are less ambiguous and more revealing if you adhere to the pencil and paper method. You'll need to develop the paper and pencil approach later on anyway, so now is a good time to start learning the practice.

Step 3. Continue to drain and write the responses for as long as new insights and revelations of the causes of the affliction appear. And keep your mind under control. It has to be quiet when doing things like this.

Step 4. Finish the draining exercise by closing off the chakras and allow them to fill with fresh energy from the crown chakra.

If you desire, you can continue the healing as follows:

Step 1. Open up the self-healing and escape channels in the crown chakra by relaxing the area on the top of your head, and allow the healing energy to flow throughout your body, flushing it and the old illness-related energy back out the escape channel. Continue until you no longer feel or observe "old" energy leaving your system.

Step 2. Close all the chakras, but leave the crown chakra open. It will close on its own when the time is right.

AUDIO TECHNOLOGY AND MEDITATION

Audio technology can aid in reaching deep meditative states allowing personal growth or exploration of the nonphysical world without having to spend years in cloistered contemplative poses. The essential technique plays a separate tone in each ear so that each hemisphere of the brain processes the tones separately. When these tones are close in frequency, you become aware of a "beat" as the brain hemispheres synchronize and begin to communicate the tone information between themselves.

Researchers studying the brainwave patterns of meditating monks developed audio tracks using these hemispherical synchronization techniques that rapidly establish and maintain the same patterns. The results using this technology are rapid and spectacular, accomplishing in a matter of a few months of practice what it takes traditional full-time monks years to attain.

The biggest problem for most using this approach to meditation is in adjusting personal schedules to allow an uninterrupted hour or so a day to listen to the programs. No special equipment is required—you need only a pair of stereo headphones, a CD player, and a comfortable chair or recliner. Your total effort is simply to listen and observe, allowing whatever happens to happen... without thought from your mind as much as possible.

Two such "audio assisted meditation" programs that have withstood the test of time are the Gateway Wave program from the Monroe Institute and the Holosync Audio Technology from the Centerpointe Research Institute. The Monroe Gateway Wave program is more traditional in its approach while the heavily marketed Centerpointe product includes bonus CDs and other materials. The web addresses for each of these organizations is listed in the Appendix.

Either program will quickly speed your meditational growth.

CHAPTER 3

ENERGY AND CONSCIOUSNESS

As far as the laws of mathematics refer to reality, they are not certain; and as far as they are certain, they do not refer to reality...reality is merely an illusion, albeit a very persistent one.
—Albert Einstein

The metaphysical realm, particularly where it relates to consciousness, is complex and can only be touched on in the space devoted to it in this book. At first, what is presented may seem self-contradictory in some respects. This is unavoidable, and so it will inevitably require reading and re-reading, thought, and contemplation before the underlying principles being described take form. When this happens, you will develop an internal understanding of the concept, but not necessarily be able to express it coherently to others or even to yourself. This is the essence of esoteric knowledge. It cannot be expressed using language. Thus we call it knowledge of the heart.

BEGINNING TERMINOLOGY

All spiritual practices recognize that human anatomy is more than mere flesh, blood, and bone. Western religions usually refer to the non-physical part of the human being as the soul. Other traditions refer to it as a spirit or consciousness. We will term a spiritual consciousness simply as a spirit. An incarnated spirit, that is, one who through an incarnational plan becomes attached to a physical human body, is termed our "higher self," although in some cases it is actually a "higher power."

Incarnated spirits are often too large to "fit" a human being, and so it splits into two parts becoming the higher self just described and a "higher power" that represents the whole of the remaining spirit. The higher self can be called upon to provide insight, perspective, reinforcement, and support to help solve earthly issues, despite its having no awareness of the physical world or how it works.

The higher self cannot be called upon to give an unfair advantage over others, cause them to love you, or to smite your enemies, all of which would be a violation of spiritual law. (See Healing and Spiritual Law in Chapter 4.) But it can, for example, be called upon to help you do your best in whatever adventure you're involved with, or to help you solve problems that you're having trouble with.

This is not to say it has no interest in our earthly experience. It does. It will help when called upon, but it must work through the incarnational plan. This means that if the incarnational plan doesn't permit or include certain things, your higher self can't help or provide for it either.

In both the physical and nonphysical, the only function of life is to grow by gaining experience, that is, to become more fully self-aware. Although there is no time or space in the nonphysical, through increased insight and perspective, change takes place as a result of the learning experiences accomplished in the physical.

Another term closely related to this subject is that of life. The working definition that we will use is that life (and therefore consciousness at whatever level) exists in anything that reacts. This sweeping definition establishes that life exists everywhere. In the earth experience, at our level of consciousness, the most recognizable life forms are carbon-based biological beings.

Life reacts on the essential basis of individual choices made possible by self-awareness. That we may not be able to discern such awareness is not a matter to be argued here. Rather, it is given as a general principle to be explored and experienced by those with a compelling interest.

The composite definition for life is based on the following:

1. Everything in the physical universe is the result of an expression of the nonphysical consciousness principle.
2. Therefore, everything in the physical universe has a direct non-physical intent governing the role it is playing.

3. While in the physical, being reflective of the incarnating spirits, life everywhere is but a symbol of the intent that expressed it.

DEFINING THE NONPHYSICAL

The line separating the physical and nonphysical realms, the veil, marks both the beginning and the end of existence in the physical. Manifestation into the physical universe as a human begins as a potential or possibility in the nonphysical. When the concept or principle to be used is completed, i.e. the incarnational plan is completed, it is manifest into the physical by passing through the veil and attaching itself to a newborn child, the choice of which is well-suited for this particular role.

The veil is a term long used to describe the separation between the physical and metaphysical. It acts as a portal without dimension that passes energy, consciousness, and awareness between the nonphysical and physical. The veil, even though dimensionless, covers the entire physical universe. Thus all matter and energy in the physical universe are in constant contact with the veil and through it, its nonphysical counterpart. It is important to understand that the veil is only a philosophical concept and does not physically exist except as a metaphor describing its function.

Our higher selves have no knowledge of what the physical universe or its problems are like. Our higher self is typically a small part of our higher power. Thus we have two spirits of considerable perspective with a vested interest in our incarnation. The human consciousness is constrained by incarnational factors established prior to incarnating and birth. Communication with our higher self must travel through the veil and the incarnational filter. Thus, there are often preplanned restrictions of both subject matter and the possible higher self responses.

Philosophically, the nonphysical world isn't "some other place" as there is no time or space in that realm. Rather, we look at the physical universe as a particular field of expressed possibility that is formed and maintained from within the nonphysical.

Our view of the nonphysical universe is the result of the duality of our thought. We think by comparing "things," and if there isn't a "thing" on which a comparison can be made, our minds *create* a thing to satisfy it. (See Rational Thought, below) Thus, we in the physical universe don't

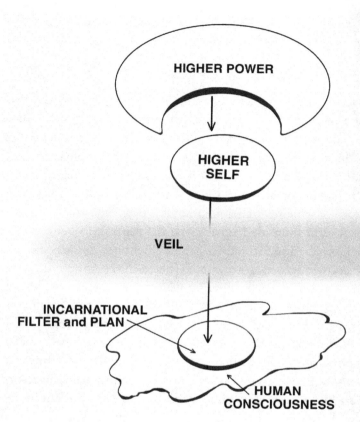

Drawing 3-1 Human consciousness and the higher power. The veil marks the interface between the physical and nonphysical realms. Our conscious-ness, while in the physical, can communicate with our higher self. It can be asked for assistance in solving earthly problems, but can do this only through the veil and incarnational plan which separates physical knowl-edge from that of the higher self.

know if the nonphysical is simply an abstraction of the mind, or whether the nonphysical universe is the "real universe" and the physical universe that we live in is the "phantom" one.

One of the early Egyptian metaphysical discoveries was that all of nature and the universe is contained within man. It is exemplified in both physical and symbolic form in Egyptian temple design, climaxing with the temples at Luxor.

Our rational thought pattern precludes conscious awareness of all of this, of course. Not only does the veil normally limit our awareness to only that within the physical universe, but further restrictions are also imposed through our incarnational plans. Limitations of our five physical senses, native abilities and talents provide the final restrictions that bring focus to and our awareness of "reality" and matters within the physical realm in general and our earth experience in particular.

The purpose of energy at our level as humans is to act as an agent of change. As change can only affect awareness, energy is useful only as a tool for learning. The learning that takes place in the physical follows the same pattern described for healing as a growth experience. Every lifetime includes many learning lessons, some run concurrently, and others consecutively. Each lifetime follows the pattern shown in Drawing 4-2 in Chapter 4.

Experience is formed when an energy principle introduces insight that increases perspective to a consciousness. This is accomplished by adding, merging or taking away a particular energy principle. This inevitably results in a change of perspective and thus a change in the perceived reality. This principle is our life learning process and the energies that are picked up, modified or dropped concretize our life-learning lessons.

The spiritual basis (or function) of the physical universe is to utilize an energy form or principle that ultimately enhances awareness. In the human consciousness metaphor, our initial awareness is who we were when we incarnated. It widens as life proceeds and experiences who we have become as a result of these changes. The experience of life thus heightens the awareness of self, and it is this new awareness that travels back through the veil to rejoin our spiritual essence upon death.

REALITY

Reality is an energy field, parts of which can be picked up through our five senses. In this way, our reality is made up only from the sensations of these senses. No two persons can experience the same reality because it is formed through their own set of five senses. Each of us always experiences our own private reality. Even though a group of people may share a common *experience*, everyone in the group still has their own reality (thus view) of that experience. Reality is time-sensitive, flowing with time in and around each of us, moment through moment.

Thus we constantly experience a new and different reality even if we are very still and not moving at all. It is in the realm of reality that our requests and desires are cast to our higher self and higher power. When objects of our desire are granted, they are gathered up and sent to us through reality. It is up to us, the requester, to recognize reality's presentation of these desires which may come in a way other than as a direct answer to our request. If the timing and conditions are right, they will show up in the physical world and be presented to us through any number of ways and circumstances.

Sometimes requests, desirable things, or situations flow past us while we are distracted by other happenings in the physical world. These then become "lost opportunities." Unfortunately, it is not possible to "go back in reality" to capture such losses. The flow of reality, like time itself, cannot be reversed, so it is not possible to "relive" or "recapture" things in past realities. The closest we have to that is (possibly) memory recall of those lost realities.

It takes time to record a memory of whatever we perceive as reality, and since reality is constantly in motion, the best we can do is to take a series of mental snapshots of it as it flows by. And so, most of reality is not recorded or remembered. Further, it is entirely possible for an event to take place in the reality field while a previous moment is being stored in memory. Of course, such an event would have to take place and complete very quickly, but when this happens, we are oblivious to that event and have no recall of it.

Because our reality is formed by the sensations of our five senses, reality itself is not recordable, nor can it be sensed by instrumentation. Any attempt to record it simply establishes a new reality stream, one that includes the attempted recording.

THE INCARNATION PRINCIPLE

The incarnational principle is basic to the functioning of the physical universe and applies universally to all life forms. Were this principle not in place, the earth would serve no purpose and would cease to exist as we presently know it. As the spiritual values used for an incarnation play out their role in real life, those living the earth experience, difficult as it is, yield rapid spiritual growth.

In many ways, the relationship between an incarnating spirit and the physical is like a hand wearing a glove. The hand in the glove is the incarnating spirit, and the glove is the physical side of the veil. Consider how the glove limits the sensations your hand can experience. As your "glove" gets older and thinner, it finally wears out, you take it off, and the incarnation is over.

This example shows how your higher self learns. Notice that your higher self only "sees" energy relationships. It has no idea of the reality experienced throughout the incarnation. It doesn't know a chair from a bicycle. But it can send you insight and perspective that will help you tell the difference.

The incarnation principle was established as a means to allow higher level spirits to accelerate their growth through their inhabitation of lower physical beings. This principle provides spiritual learning and growth by deliberately limiting and restricting the consciousness of the incarnating spirits (our souls) to a small subset of their actual essence, as witnessed through the human body.

Upon death, the incarnated spirit, our higher self—now more aware of its attributes in this expanded form—returns to its true essence as a fully nonphysical entity, and rejoins your higher power, becoming one again. There is no other agenda or hidden purpose embedded in this principle.

Prior to the start of any incarnation, the spirit is free to choose any genus of an appropriate species level that fits it. There is no "backtracking" into a level below its spiritual capability since that learning has already taken place and is completed. Likewise, moving to a more complex species before sufficient learning has taken place will probably lead to a short and tragic life.

Within a given species, there is a range of physical variances such as size, weight, and dexterity. In the case of humans, different capabilities are needed for the many lifestyles, occupations, and activities available to be lived. Athletes, for example, require very physical, energetic bodies, while college professors, office workers, and particularly writers of books such as this, need bodies that can tolerate long hours of physical inactivity and drudgery.

The Incarnation

The body *is* the spiritual incarnation in the physical, and the marriage of body and spirit forms a link and an immutable agreement to proceed with the life. This marriage can take place prior to birth or can be delayed as long as two or three years. But once the link is formed it can only be broken by the death of the body in the physical.

The purpose of the incarnational plan is to limit and control the specifics of self under study by the incarnating spirit. The life experiences are immutably restricted to those aspects allowed by the plan. Once the plan is in place, the incarnation plays out the game of life. The incarnating spirit—the higher self—controls the progress through the animation energy provided by it. This energy, known to healers as life energy, is the sustaining force of the incarnation.

In many ways, life using the earth experience is difficult. The question to be answered is in life how well you handled yourself and what you learned using your fettered assets. Winning the fight is not the measure of success that we're looking for in the metaphysical sense. Rather, it is about what we learned about our self during the execution of the fight.

Life as an Experiment

This is why life is called an experiment. Some learning plans take many lifetimes to complete, while others but one or even a fraction. Incarnations fall into two general types, the most common being a growth or change incarnation. The other, the validation incarnation, is used to validate and concretize prior learning and growth. Those using a growth incarnation tend to be planners and goal-oriented. They might even stay at one occupation for their entire working life.

Validation incarnations tend to be free-ranging, with little patience for protocol and procedure since the goal is to validate past achievements and move on. This is a much more difficult incarnation than a growth incarnation that has established goals. Those living a validation life have no fixed goals, few attachments, and typically fewer really close friends. They feel free to move on to new pursuits with nary a tear as soon as they are satisfied with whatever they were doing.

There is no hierarchy between the two incarnational models, for as soon as a validation incarnation, which also may take several lifetimes to complete, is finished, it is time to start work on a new incarnational plan that will stipulate a new set of learning experiences for use in a growth incarnation. This or else leave the earth experience for an entirely different growth experience elsewhere.

The incarnational principle is a tool for developing greater awareness of self. As such, it imposes restriction as a means of concentrating focus onto very specific, carefully selected and narrowly defined aspects of our spiritual essence which in the physical is called our "self". Life lived through incarnational restriction is thus an exploration of those incarnationally allowed aspects, and as they become understood, a new awareness of self emerges.

Achieving new self-awareness and perspective through experience is spiritual growth, an evolution that we call *healing*. The ultimate effect of healing energy stays with the recipient awareness in the form of insight or perspective at some increased level of awareness. As a rule, healing energy can stay in the physical for a short time, but only temporarily as a stored form in matter such as the chakras or crystals. (See Chapter 4, Crystal Technology.)

UNIVERSAL CONNECTION TO THE NONPHYSICAL

Relationships are the consciousnesses formed by group awareness, and follow the same life cycle pattern as ordinary individuals. When enough energy is put behind a relationship, such as in a large corporation or nation, they are said to "take on a life of their own," meaning that they become self-perpetuating. This may seem the case, but like all life, these "super-consciousnesses" follow the primal directive to survive and grow. And like all life, they follow the same inevitable path into decline and obscurity in the sands of history.

An alternative illustration more clearly illustrates the connection between the physical and nonphysical realms and the "size" relationship between the two. Drawing 3-2 also shows the physical world as a three-dimensional figure resting on the infinite expanse of the non-physical veil. Being symbolic of each other there is really no distinction between the physical and nonphysical as they essentially are one and the same. Thus there is intimate contact between everything in the physical and nonphysical, separated only by the veil.

The physical, to use a rational description, only exists as a specialized field within the nonphysical realm. The two, being symbolic of the principles they express, are symbols of each other. As such, they are identical and yet different and separate. Such is the limitation of our descriptive language.

Learning and healing, at the incarnational level, are interrelated, thus always go hand in hand. When a life learning experience is accepted, one's balance or equilibrium is upset. Acceptance of the lesson as such isn't something most of us are actually aware of. However uncomfortable the lesson, agreement to accept the experience at some level is always the first step toward growth. As healing takes place, *i.e.* learning with new perspectives, balance and thus comfort is gradually restored, concretizing the learning experience and locking in the growth just achieved.

From the rational perspective, awareness and the reality it reveals are heavily intertwined. At first, there seems no way to break into the chain of these self-defining concepts. The problem is compounded by our thought modality, the way we think and interpret reality, for it defines our perception. And it is perception that gives us our awareness and its connection with reality. Our perceived reality is as much a product of interpretation as it is of what our senses report. This makes our understanding of the true nature of reality, even within the limited confines detected and resolved by our five senses, dubious at best. Such is the nature of the human consciousness.

CONSCIOUSNESS

The metaphysical principle behind consciousness, particularly that of the human level, defies rational explanation or description, and no attempt will be made to provide a succinct definition of consciousness. Dictionaries are of no help as consciousness and awareness are used to

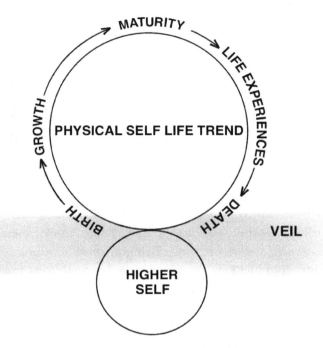

MATURITY

LIFE EXPERIENCES

GROWTH

PHYSICAL SELF LIFE TREND

BIRTH

DEATH

VEIL

HIGHER
SELF

*Drawing 3-2 The earth experience starts with birth at the veil and pro-
gresses clockwise as shown through the earth experiences, i.e. birth, physical
experiences and finally death. At death our higher self rejoins our higher
power through the veil taking with it the new perspectives learned during this
lifetime, thus making the life experience complete.*

define each other, hence a circular definition.

When describing this subject, I generally prefer to use *consciousness* or
spirit as a proactive nonphysical being. Although it still leaves unanswered
what consciousness is, at least spirit is a more familiar term that often better conveys the essence of what is intended. Also, it is somewhat easier to
describe an *awareness* as something that is possessed by a consciousness. In
our lexicon, the term consciousness implies a specific nonphysical being
whereas an awareness indicates a condition of that consciousness.

Thus we can make a distinction between consciousness and awareness
by stating that awareness is a trait peculiar to a consciousness. Note that
when someone loses consciousness, they also lose awareness, although

awareness can continue in spite of a loss of consciousness. Those who have suffered a near-death experience report a continued awareness of their surroundings even though their body is apparently "dead" as they float around.

Others, while under anesthesia during surgery, sometimes report episodes of moving around the operating room and taking short trips throughout the hospital. Anesthesiologists have discovered that those under anesthesia still have normal brain activity, responding to light flashes throughout the surgery. So far, no one has discovered "where we go" when we are anesthetized.

As a concept, everything in creation is a form of conscious expression, and thus, consciousness is all that exists. Pure consciousness has no dimension, no time and no thought. Pure consciousness is one of simple existence, a state of being. Being at once anything, everything, and nothing. And lucky us, we are advanced enough to at least be *aware* of our consciousness.

INTRODUCTION TO ENERGY

As a term, energy has application in both the physical and metaphysical worlds. The usual definition of energy is something that can do something or cause something to happen. Energy causes things to move, ovens to heat, televisions to work, and cars to run. In common usage, energy is often confused with its source of fuel such as gasoline, electricity or heat. Fuels as such all release energy, but energy itself is not defined except in these terms.

Energy in metaphysical terms is a substance that follows a fixed energetic principle that can evoke change. It is a universal operative, that is, it functions in the same manner in both the physical and nonphysical. Once manifest and placed in motion by intent, energy is not intelligent, reasoning, or mutable, as it can only act within the narrowly defined limits dictated by its endowing principle.

Energy consists of a vector that grades its relevancy to an object and a reactive principle that defines its range of action. We use the term object as something energy might operate on. All objects are thus opportunities for fulfillment of an energy principle. Energy of itself is not capable of growth or change of venue, although it can, by rendering insight or change, release a second energy principle as a response to its fulfillment.

THE SYMBOL

As healers, the importance of our meaning of symbol cannot be over-

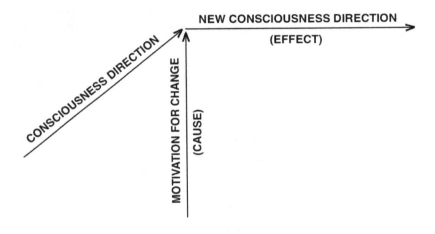

Drawing 3-3 Cause and effect—the direction of a consciousness flow is affected (changed) by an energetic principle (a cause) resulting in a new direction for that consciousness.

emphasized. The term itself is of Greek origin, *symbolon*, translated as a sign by which one knows or infers a thing, or to throw or put together. This has largely evolved into the popular meaning of equivalence, that is, a symbol represents an idea or a physical object. But in philosophical terms, the meaning goes in a different direction, as a sign of recognition formed by two parts of an object which are brought together to make it whole. This is much closer to the original Greek meaning.

In the sense that we as healers use the word, a symbol is not a representative equivalency of an object. In fact, it is nearly the opposite: it is the object. Our view is that a symbol resonates with the object, allowing it to function as a surrogate for the object it represents once a linkage is formed between them. Although philosophically a symbol is often viewed as that from which it came, in the healer's lexicon that is not actually the case. Neither the object nor the symbol representing it is linked until an energy principle establishes the connection between them. This is the basis of Reiki 2's absent healing protocol.

In the metaphysical or healing sense, the symbol both maintains and is maintained by a link across the veil between it and the nonphysical essence of the object it is from, or what it represents as an energy form. When we activate the link, the symbol and the object resonate and become one through that connection. Thus the symbol becomes the object just as the object becomes the symbol.

The indelible linkage between physical symbol and its spiritual consciousness is more concrete than ethereal. As healers, when we describe symbolic linkages, we are talking about a connection between a symbol and its nonphysical manifestation. The link is a pathway connecting the two objects along which energy can be directed to flow in either direction. Thus, a symbol has a distinctive meaning to energy healers far beyond an insignia or some other emblematic representation.

And so the connection between the physical universe and the nonphysical realm. Because of the spiritual essence of all in the physical and the incarnation principle at play, the symbolic linkage to spirit is the spiritual principle that creates the reality that we perceive through our awareness of self. As we live our lives and explore our physical nature, we also explore our spiritual or nonphysical side as well.

DEATH IN THE PHYSICAL

The energy flow through the veil can only be withdrawn by the spirit supporting it. Death comes when an affliction or injury makes the body untenable, or the present life's learning lessons and incarnational plan are completed. When the life energy flow is stopped, the conscious awareness expressed in the physical ceases to be manifest.

When the human consciousness is withdrawn through the veil, the body de-animates and dies although lower conscious levels within the body may de-manifest at any time without apparent ill effect. This happens all the time as various cells mature, become defective and die. More serious physical effects take place when elements supporting the senses or vital organs are withdrawn due to accident or disease. This results in physical infirmity and without successful human intervention may ultimately make the entire body unviable, resulting in death.

Reasons for flow termination vary, but are always driven—or at least allowed—by the incarnational plan. On the physical side, they include non-viability of body functionality due to any of a multitude of physical causes such as age, sickness or injury. On the nonphysical side, examples include the life irreversibly not going in the appropriate or anticipated direction, thus not yielding the intended experience for the incarnation. Termination of life after the experience being sought was obtained is another possibility. And in other cases "death by chance or accident" takes place as simply another learning experience as far as the incarnational plan is concerned.

Typically the process of the de-manifestation starts by the highest level of consciousness withdrawing, thus signaling the oncoming death of the body. Death at the lower levels usually follows in stages over a period of minutes, hours, or days, thus allowing time to surgically obtain organs for transplanting into another body. The Tibetan tradition as related in *The Tibetan Book of the Dead* is that full de-manifestation takes three days.

FOCUS

Focus describes the organization of intent, the equivalent of "aiming" in the physical. Focus also works like a magnifying glass—the stronger it is, the more detailed and specifically targeted the intent can be brought to bear on a given object. Or, with a weaker lens (less focus), you can see a larger part of the picture but with less detail.

The focus center is an important feature of the nonphysical human anatomy because it serves two distinct purposes in everyday life and is used all the time. First and foremost, it is the means by which we narrow and direct the attention of our awareness. It is also a part of the center that radiates our conscious identity throughout reality and thereby attracting things into our lives that we want and need.

In physical terms, this means that for a given strength or ability, focus makes the intensity of the intent greater if it is concentrated. Poorly focused intent spreads the energy over a wider area making it less effi-

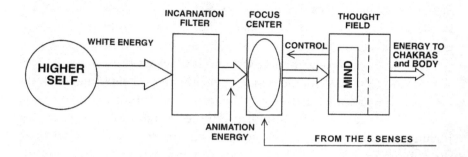

Drawing 3-4 White broadband energy from our higher power (or higher self) first passes through our incarnation filter. It is then passed through the focus center that is controlled by our mind. Next, focused energy is passed on to our thought field and mind before becoming our animation energy source. Inputs from our five physical senses are also fed to the thought field and define our reality. Naturally, our mind does its best to prevent sharp focus, so the practice of stopping its thoughts—mind noise and clutter—is a good idea.

cacious. Only a consciousness can create and project intent, and so in the metaphysic focused intent is the harbinger of a targeted conscious exchange of energy.

It should be remembered that our physical hands, so often used to supply healing Reiki energy, are merely physical points of focus in this context. As such their use is unneeded and easily bypassed once proper use of our focus center is achieved through Reiki 2 training and after much experience.

Although absent healing can give the healer more flexibility, the psychology of physical touch while healing gives an important physical sense of process and participation to those being healed. Thus healing by touch is an important aspect that reinforces the healing process.

Advanced healers learn to use the focus center to concentrate healing energy at a given location in a given place and time. With careful practice, focus can be mentally picked up and moved around on a given object. The focus center is used for both Reiki 1 and Reiki 2 healing energies, and so those with only Reiki 1 training can still practice and enhance their focusing and healing skills while healing by touch.

The focus center also lets others know who we are by radiating our identity signature into reality space. This signal, which can consciously be masked and hidden, brings people and things into our lives that we have requested or, as an incarnational matter, need. (Quartz crystals easily capture the radiated identity signal and store it. This is the reason that healers using crystals typically avoid allowing others to handle their crystals.)

Targeted intent is important for those who heal, for without it, our healing ability is disappointingly low. Advanced healers take great care in aligning their intent with that of the receiver. Far from an intellectual exercise, highly focused and carefully targeted intent is used whenever an energy healing is to take place.

Change resulting from an energy exchange takes place under two conditions. When dealing with physical matter which to us is of an unconscious but reactive nature, intent is blindly accepted by the object. This makes the earth or stones ideal receptors for draining energy and grounding exercises. Otherwise, energy received tends to alter in some way the life path the receiver is presently on.

In the nonphysical, where change affects a spiritual awareness, healing energy is packaged as one of four distinctive principles useful for healers. These energy principles, mentioned earlier, are called insight, perspective, reinforcement, and support. Other energy types exist but will not be described as they have little bearing on the healing art.

Healing energy has many possible manifestations aside from the actual mending of spirit and body. It is not restricted to just making some biological influence. As its work can be directed toward every consciousness level, its influence can be felt in the physical as changes in awareness, life quality, and living conditions. Given the right conditions, our reality can be changed in the blink of an eye as the consciousnesses respond to their changed awareness. Except for the exclusions instilled by spiritual law and incarnational plan stipulations, there is no special limitation on what changes in perception nonphysical energy can instill.

Energies of different levels, although sharing the common energetic principle of change, manifest according to their relationship within the environment where they are at cause. Thus, the apparent effect of a particular energy changes with the conditions under which intent is received or enabled to be manifest.

Probably the most frequent issue evoking inconsistency is that of poorly focused intent. Intent, sharply focused, is always appropriate. Beginning healers should spend time learning to quickly bring on tightly controlled focus.

SYMBOLIC THINKING

Unlike rational thought, symbolic thinking dominated ancient mentality and probably that of most uncontaminated indigenous cultures of today. This thought process tends to evaluate all sensory input and memory simultaneously, summing them into a single value or symbol. Pure symbolic thought is about the essence of reality rather than the value as expressed by the rational thought process.

Symbolic presentation situates the entire meaning of the present moment into a "thought ball" that cannot be disassembled. As such, the meaning is encoded and encapsulated in the symbol with no reference to language. This symbol is presented as a whole to the consciousness, which tends to respond to it as an automatic reaction to the present environment.

To the rational mind, such an "automatic" response is as puzzling as the symbolic analysis itself. Symbolic responses come into today's human awareness as a series of "flashes" of inspiration, recognition, or knowledge. This can only happen during those brief intervals when rational thought is not dominant.

In a twinkling, there is total comprehension of the thought ball contents. For most without practice and training to capture such thoughts, that same comprehension and understanding can vanish seconds later unless the person receiving it is ready for it, while possibly being in a meditative state. Without such readiness, less than a minute after the thought ball arrives, only a vague memory is left that "something" occurred.

The sensation is that of an "instant" dream. For those not trained in responding in only seconds after the dream completes, the memory of its content is largely gone and a minute or two later there is essentially no recollection that it even happened. The contents of the thought ball never reach our short-term memory without considerable practice and readiness to accept it.

Reality seen through symbolic thought smoothly flows, not from moment to moment as in its rational experience, but "moment through moment." There are no gaps or missing elements in the reality of the symbolic mind, and so the mental image of it is tightly focused on what the present moment is, rather than what it once was or could be sometime in the future. As a result, those who predominantly use symbolic thought have greater instinctive or innate sensitivity to the nature around them than most of us living in a modern civilization.

Rational thought cannot handle the present moment because it takes time to evaluate an instant. By the time rational processing of a moment is finished, that moment is long gone along with many more, and so memory and additional interpretive logic are used to integrate and fill in the intervals between the moments that are sampled.

Thus the key to quieting the rational mind is revealed. By remaining in the moment, there is no opportunity for its analysis and merciless mind chatter to intrude and disrupt the true experience of reality.

RATIONAL THOUGHT

The reality in which we live is an energy field bounded by our thought modality, which for most of us living the earth experience today happens to be rational thought. Rational thought is a biological function based in the mind, itself a logical function that lives and dies with the brain.

The mind operates entirely by comparison. For example, if you see a white ball, rational thought immediately tells you that there is a black ball, even if it has never seen a black ball and for all it knows, there never has been a black ball. This illustrates the so-called *duality* of thought. In other words, for a complete understanding of an image, it must be viewed from both itself and its opposite. This characteristic thought pattern is a by-product of rational thinking.

The brain is controlled by a complex set of chemicals released by the body as its response to the reality surrounding it. This is not always the same reality that our mind sees, as the body's logic and response to our five senses is not bounded by the duality of thought that our rational mind indicates is before us.

Our human understanding is limited to a specific range of experiences through the metaphor of physical life as interpreted by rational logic. Physical life, as we are aware of it, is first constrained by the five senses. These severely limit our view of the reality around us, and after them, our rationality further mollifies its extent. This yields a peculiar and self-limiting form of awareness.

And so it becomes that personal reality, that is, the reality that we as individuals experience, is really a matter of perception taken at a particular level of awareness and thought pattern. But after removing all bounds on human awareness, in the final analysis, true reality is everything, something incomprehensible and quite unimaginable to our rational thought patterns.

Roughly 4,500 years ago, rational thought became a possibility for all as written languages became widespread. Both written and spoken language demands distinction of concept because it, and the rational thought that defines it, situates every expression at a time and place. It is a sequential form of expression that demands a step-by-step analysis of contrasting values of each term, rather than the simultaneous integrated view provided by the symbolic thought patterns that came before.

Rational thought breaks up the smooth flow of reality, reducing it into steps, some small, some large. We have no direct sense of either time or space since both are outside reality. Even so, these inferred concepts whose gaps in reality are neatly filled in by the mind and placed into our awareness by pure rational thought are seemingly real. Depending on one's viewpoint, rational thought pulls us out of the moment during the time it takes to process and infer, or symbolic thought pulls us out of time and space. In either case, it is a matter of perspective.

Rational thought is limited in its expression ability because it is based on a small dictionary of native terms in an unconscious dictionary of concepts that we are all born with. All thought and understanding in our rational awareness are based on those concepts contained in this minimal reference work. Our languages, sciences, and philosophies, hopes, dreams and desires are expressed with words whose compounded meanings eventually reduce to circular definitions beyond which our written and unabridged dictionaries can go no further.

There are no "new" fundamental conceptual words being invented as we might believe. After all, new words are constantly being added to our dictionaries. It is the case that all the words of our written language, including the so-called new ones, are only abbreviations for collections of predefined words whose "meanings" ultimately defy analysis by the rational mind. The words in our dictionaries merely infer undefined concepts and linguistic shortcuts found in that base set of meanings biologically instilled in the human brain. These "base word concepts" are linked to our various languages, enabling speech and rational thought. However, they cannot be rationally explored or defined since they don't refer to each other and there are no meanings to compare them to, something the rational mind requires to "work."

In practice, rational language has a tendency to create words of shaded meanings that are defined using words that are "equivalent but simpler." These, in turn, are defined with even simpler words. For example, if an ordinary word is followed through successive definitions of the words defining it, usually by the third or fourth generation the "bottom" of the dictionary is reached, and the definitions turn circular.

Thus the process fails when there is finally a need to define the essence of an object. Essence cannot be described or explained by simplifying a word. Nor can a concept or principle. This breakdown in rational logic is easy to understand because in order to simplify a term, a comparison to something, either known or made up, must be made.

At some point, there is nothing left to compare, and no simpler term can be divined by our rational logic. The only rational recourse is to attempt definition through allegory, metaphor, and parable. Or make up something to compare. For this reason, rational thought can never discover, be completely original, or communicate the true essence of a term.

Rational thought and tightly focused awareness slows down the perception of reality and distributes it to our awareness across time. As such, it is a "low-speed" form of awareness heavily dependent on memory. When details are of interest, we can further narrow our focus to present increasingly smaller components of our reality, giving finer resolution on points of interest, but as explained earlier, only at the expense of not seeing the complete picture.

Symbolic thinking, on the other hand, continuously—and simultaneously—brings into our awareness all the information from our senses, often accompanied with additional insight and perspective. No conscious analysis or thought is associated with symbolic "thinking." When using this thought modality, all senses are processed into a single value or symbol that smoothly changes with the flow of reality.

RATIONALITY AS SEQUENTIAL LOGIC

As has been hinted before, language is a limitation when dealing with the metaphysic. Indeed, language is a natural adjunct to our rationality. Both require the inferred concepts of time and space. Rational thought and knowledge are expressed through language in a sequential manner, syllable after syllable, word after word until a completed thought is expressed. The memory supporting our rational functions maintains the continuity of expression over the time the thought is being expressed, is spoken, is being heard, or written down.

Rational thinking is implemented as a sequential form of logic that expects and demands that a cause always precedes an effect. When the rational mind runs into an effect without a logical or an inferred cause, it remains baffled or suspends the rules of physical reality in that regard and uses the miracle or magic as a way to explain the mystery.

Once the miracle principle, however illogical it may be, is invoked, logic is "restored" and the rational mind is satisfied that all is in order. No rationality is removed when the miracle is used as a part of logic; it is simply augmented to reach a conclusion without logical gaps.

A miracle is nothing more than a rational ploy to suspend physical reality so that supernatural or divine action can be "logically" used to explain. Miracles are established through any number of mechanisms, all of which fall in the belief category ranging from pure illusional magic to divine intervention. In the past, mysterious unseen forces such as gods, devils, and magic powers were given credit for causing the miracle or curse being examined. The only requirement for a miracle is that the power effecting it remain unseen and beyond mortal man, or at least the self. Faith, belief, and superstition are the precursors to the miracle.

However well-intentioned or carefully applied, rational logic is essentially a flawed logic, one that cannot always be trusted. Because our rationality and its penchant for inferred conclusions are not always based on fact or confirmed existence, its conclusions are always suspect.

Rational thought has a problem when it comes to energy healers. After all, how can someone cause healing or relief by simply touching the afflicted, or worse still, how can drawing unfathomable symbolic things in the air possibly affect someone miles or continents away? Healers, particularly those new to Reiki or other energy healing methods, must initially operate on blind trust that "something good will happen" as they work their methods. Advanced healers deal with the rational thought problem by stopping the mind's constant chatter.

THE DUALITY OF RATIONAL THOUGHT

The rational mind attacks reality relentlessly, looking for contrast and oversimplification through the systematic dissection of everything reported by the five senses. Every rational thought begins with a distinction of what it sees, and if there is no record or memory of an opposite, an assumption of that opposite is made and treated as if it were real. This is the basis of rational duality.

As the beginning basis of our logic, a logic that operates only through comparison, if facts are not in evidence, they are generated on the spot as needed then treated as real. Rational thought, unless carefully managed, is not trustworthy. The assumptions it makes may not exist in reality, and when taken as real over a period of time, can render a chaotic life.

We have no rational means for differentiating assumptions or facts unless each is independently tested. Thus, we cannot know from face value which assumptions are valid and which are questionable. For this reason, it is sometimes difficult to positively establish what is real and what is not unless the object can be physically tested and observed through our five physical senses.

The source of the philosophical "duality" is rational thought in action. Rational duality gives us many commonplace but opposing concepts such as good and evil, positive and negative, yin and yang. Rational logic always deals with the comparison of two objects; sometimes they're real and physical, other times completely ethereal.

REALITY IS CONSTRAINED BY RATIONAL THOUGHT AND THE FIVE PHYSICAL SENSES

Our five senses are normally passed on to our rational mind and stored in memory along with tags indicating a time and location as well as other information about the environment of the moment. To the rational mind, reality consists of only what it picks up through these senses and our various tools and inventions that extend our range of sensitivities. Although we have no direct sensory input for either space or time, the rational mind categorizes all of its perceptions on this basis. For this reason, our conceptual view of space and time is said to be inferred or imaginary.

The rational mind acknowledges that our senses have limitations, and it knows that it fills in gaps in our sensor range with unproven inferences, approximations, and guesses. Even so, it continues to deny that there is anything more to reality than has already been experienced and witnessed. Since the mind's fabricated reality is key to our waking awareness, we cannot be absolutely sure of anything that we perceive through our five senses, although life experiences make us "pretty sure" of what is before us.

True reality is a flowing energy field of infinite size. It is from sensing this field that our five senses make up our reality of the moment. Reality is not something that can be shared by others because no two people can occupy the same place and time from which "a" reality is sampled. Thus, we all have our own special reality—a separate and personal view of it from which we base our daily lives. And so we all see life from a different perspective of reality.

The totality of reality even within the physical universe is not accessible to human consciousnesses living the incarnated earth experience. The conventional view of reality is that it is determined by the obvious limitations of temperature, climate and other environmental conditions

AWARENESS

A way to craft our way into understanding awareness through the consciousness principle is to rationalize that since creation had a beginning, then once it did not exist, and that something caused it to become. Rational thinking cannot tolerate uniqueness, and so it immediately infers that in the nothingness, a cause appeared that caused creation to happen.

Although this seems logical, these inferences produce two impossible states. First, it assumed that there was once a time when nothing existed. But if a state of nothing once existed, then neither could a cause. And so the question: "If nothing existed, where did the cause that created creation come from?" This difficulty exists because our rationality insists on a chronologically based thought pattern. And since time is also an inferred concept, the argument is on even shakier legs.

This is our rational thought at work, where all concept, thought, evaluation, and thereby our human awareness is based on the comparison of two objects in an inferred time field. The rational foundation obliges and binds us to an understanding that because consciousness exists, non-consciousness must also exist. This leads us to an abyss where "things" may not be there, but there is awareness of them. Rational thought and its comparison logic have its problems for it is "always correct" even when its solution is totally wrong or wrong for you.

where the human body can thrive or at least briefly survive. The qualities of our individual human body further restrict our range of physical experience, and within this range, the sensitivities of our physical senses instill further physical limitations.

Our five senses do not present a contiguous sample of the reality that surrounds us. Taste is limited, for example, to only that part of true reality that can be placed on the tongue. With practice, we can narrow and sharpen our focus allowing us to individually peer deeper into various aspects of our consciousness one sense at a time. But such focus reduces the overall view that we have in exchange for that detail. In this sense, focus gives an increasingly false sense of reality although it allows one to peer closer into that which makes up our personal reality.

Explicitly defining consciousness remains a lofty and largely unnecessary goal. As long as rational thinking is applied to the subject, there is a structural consistency that can be discerned, but exactly what it is that makes up that structure is a mystery. Or at least it is beyond our language and rational thought to relate.

Higher levels of consciousness are not rationally logical, but they have a discernible hierarchy based on nonphysical levels and principles that can be manifest into the physical as symbols. Thus, all we see and experience around us are but symbols, resonances amongst our personality expressed as a principle, those in our societal circle and within all creation.

The Higher Self

The higher self is the consciousness (or spirit) that incarnated with us as we entered the physical world. The spirit it comes from is often quite large, far too large to "fit" into a human. And so only a part of that spirit, our "higher self," becomes our incarnational companion. As incarnated beings, we still have an unbreakable bond to that spirit—that portion of our self that did not incarnate—from which we came. We call that spirit our "higher power" as compared to our incarnating spirit, our higher self.

It should be noted that in those instances where the higher power can fit the human mold, it serves as both the higher self and at the same time, the higher power.

Because our higher self has a stake in our incarnational outcome, it is a valuable resource and can help us by sending insight, perspective, support, and reinforcement using symbolic "thought balls" to help us solve problems whenever asked. Our higher self has no concept of time or space and knows nothing about the details of living a life in the physical. However, having a vested interest in the incarnation, it operates as a "senior partner" and is always available as a resource, even though it cannot directly influence the reality that each of us faces in our daily life.

Facing reality is our job.

The gifts from our higher self help us resolve issues that, at first, seem insurmountable and for which we've asked for assistance. Such support comes in the form of complete "ideas" that simply pop into our minds. Thoughts from our higher self cannot directly "talk" to us since it has no rational "thought" ability. Further, your higher self has no memory, only insight and perspective.

So communication with it doesn't seem like it comes from "anywhere." It is just an idea that flows into our awareness complete and without analysis, unlike other ideas come to mind as a sequence of thought. Such sequential revelations are the product of our rational mind.

Communication with our higher self is not difficult and has no particular protocol. But it helps if you can find a quiet, comfortable place to be for the time you want to spend phrasing and asking your questions.

Start by quieting your mind, as it will be of little help at this stage. Next start to formulate your request, using your mind as little as you can. This part of the process is meant to help you clearly focus on your problem, and once you understand it, form the intent to ask your higher self for insight and perspective that will help you solve the problem.

Your request might go something like this: "Give me what is necessary to understand ..." You must remember that your request must be clear. Spend some time working out the request so that it is clearly phrased to the best of your ability.

There is no need to physically speak your request, as your request will be heard through the intent you used while forming the question. Again, as much as possible keep your mind quiet as you compose the request.

Remember that your higher self is your partner and in this respect, it is bound to help you solve your issues. There is no begging or pleading necessary. Focus on the process and the clarity of your request—without as much thought as you can muster—is all that is important.

Your response will probably not immediately show up, especially not with lightning and thunder. Rather, it quietly arrives as a new insight into the problem you're working on without thought. It simply appears. Also, your answer will be what is best for you, not necessarily exactly what you want or asked for.

If you've quieted you mind sufficiently, you may suddenly start "thinking" about new ways to handle your problem. Remember that your answer will always be in the form of "instant" insight, not some new knowledge or physical action. As the received insight fades your answer is complete, and thoughts about it will naturally start to form.

If you don't feel you've heard the response, go through the process again. It takes practice to properly formulate a request and to keep your mind quiet so the response can manifest itself into your consciousness. Thinking at this time doesn't help at all, and contributes nothing but noise while you're trying to open up for a short period of time.

Here are the steps for making an insight and perspective request:

Step 1. Find a quiet, comfortable place where you won't be disturbed. You can be seated, in a meditation pose, or lying down.

Step 2. Quiet your body so you can quiet your mind. Ideally, you'll become calm and without thought, but this takes considerable practice.

Step 3. Compose your question, again without thought as much as possible.

Step 4. Form your intent that it be sent to your higher self.

Step 5. Wait quietly—again without thought as much as possible—for an insight to appear. When it appears it will seem like you just thought of the answer. The answer will appear as one complete thought, not as a sequence of thoughts. Those thoughts are from the rational mind trying to "help you."

If you don't feel you've received an answer, wait a little while then try again. Answers to requests often take some time to appear. If you're doing this near bedtime, go ahead with your normal bedtime routine. The answer may be in your head the next morning after you have slept.

This practice is thrilling. The more you ask for assistance the clearer the responses will become. And when you don't get a response, repeat your request rephrasing the question if necessary. Your success depends on accurately phrasing your request then recognizing the insight once it arrives. Be persistent with your requests. Your higher self is infinitely patient and totally non-judgmental.

CHAPTER 4

HEALING THEORY AND PRACTICE

If what is seen is portrayed in the language of logic, then it is science. If it is communicated through forms whose connections are not accessible to the conscious mind but are recognized intuitively, then it is art.

—Albert Einstein

HEALING DEFINED

We use the terms "illness" and "sickness" throughout this chapter. Sickness refers to illnesses such as the flu, and other medically related conditions that "slow you down." Illness is used as a metaphysical term, a restriction brought on by the client's behavior and incarnational plan. Illnesses in this respect, do not necessarily foster a medical condition, but they can be associated with one.

Sicknesses bound to a related illness are usually curable by gaining insight into the fundamentals of the learning lesson in play at the time. But sickness isn't necessarily related to an illness; the human body is a complex life form, and it is often the case that it "becomes sick" due to exposure to some pathogen or through accidents that are not directly related to the incarnational plan.

Healing is the release of restrictions that prevent our experience of life through an unimpeded response to reality. When we use the term "restriction", we are referring to incarnational "blocks" that are in place to guide us, gently or otherwise, toward the learning we're here to accomplish. Such blocks are dissolved when an associated life learning lesson is completed, allowing new and exciting learning lessons to be experienced.

The term "learning" leads to "knowledge" that our minds capture and (hopefully) remember while we're in a conscious state. This is the physical side of things. The metaphysical equivalent of knowledge is perspective. Thus healing is a form of applied insight that we as healers give to our clients as Reiki, Chi, Shakti, or insight by whatever name in other healing traditions.

REIKI THEORY

The difference between Reiki and placebo healings is that Reiki is a nonphysical or metaphysical healing technique while the placebo effect operates strictly in the physical. That placebo medication (so-called "sugar" pills or other inert treatments) is a powerful healing strategy on its own cannot be denied. Statistically, about one in three people given placebo medication responds well to it. However, Reiki treatments offer the placebo effect in addition to its spiritual component. This typically makes for a more potent healing experience. (See more on the placebo effect under How Reiki Works later in this chapter.)

There are several factors that can limit the "strength" of a Reiki treatment. Although Reiki 1 practitioners have received their attunement, most Reiki classes do not teach how the Reiki flow can be turned on. Nor do they teach how to sense when the flow is being accepted, or how to find the sensitive locations on the body that will accept heavy flow. And most classes do not teach spiritual law and how it affects a healing session.

Insight can be freely passed around the nonphysical realm making it a simple matter for healers to direct it towards their clients. When the timing and intent are in harmony, insight freely flows into the client from the nonphysical and truly remarkable healings can occur. However, it must be said that those suffering from purely physical sicknesses usually do not directly respond to energy healing alone. They will usually respond by becoming more calm and relaxed, more easily accepting their condition while the body heals of its own accord without the tension brought on by the anxiety concerning their condition.

Spiritual healing is about gaining the perspective that we seek as a part of our incarnational plan. Thus, it is a form of practical or "applied" spirituality. Illness should always be looked upon as a restriction of self-expression, regardless of its manifestation. Restrictions such as these are always related to the fundamentals of the life being led by the individual experiencing them and never about others. Healing is an internal, largely nonphysical process, the result of acquiring insight and perspective—experience, in other words—at some level of consciousness within our physical body. When this happens, the body will spontaneously heal of its own accord.

Healing always brings on a new level of thinking because as the insight takes effect, it introduces new perspectives at the conscious level where the healing took place. As a practice, then, the art of healing is simply one of applied insight by the healer who has no way of knowing anything about the insight actually being provided.

Also, as healers, we are usually not consciously aware of the underlying learning that is taking place in our clients, although when completed it is often revealed by the client using such expressions as, "Boy, I'll never try that one again!" or "I'm sure glad that's over." Or perhaps, "I may have learned a lot, but I never want to go through that again!"

In the final analysis, healing changes the reality of the person being healed by increasing his perspective. This is an important concept for it broadens the scope of what healing is really about and how it has application in almost every aspect of daily life. As such, healing, by its very definition, is spiritual growth, that is, fulfilling one's incarnational imperative.

ILLNESS AS A CONDITION FOR GROWTH

When viewed from a broader perspective, illness isn't just about being "sick." Restrictions in everyday life are indicative of illness, or in other words, they reveal an ongoing or pending life learning lesson. In the physical, examples of such restrictions are easy to describe. We don't graduate from school until we've gone through all the grades. We must learn to drive before we get a driver's license. Professional advancement comes only after you've learned to do the job.

Lost professional advancement opportunities, poor relations with neighbors and relatives, and even closer to home, fights or harsh words with the ones you love are examples of lessons underway. They are so common that they seem "natural," yet when the learning is finally completed, these contentious issues vanish without a whisper. Such learning is acknowledged by a reduction in stress and an inner feeling of peace.

Examples such as these show that we are given experiences at our level before we are allowed—or asked—to reach out for a greater challenge. And so it is in the metaphysic, we are never given a life learning lesson opportunity beyond our capability to succeed. This is assured as a part of our incarnational plan. We have the option to accept or reject any such learning lesson until we feel that we are ready for it. Acceptance of the lesson indicates a willingness to change and in no small way, a conquering of fear. Examples here might be an offer for a new job position, a chance to move to a new city, or even a marriage proposal. When declined, the lesson is put off, and the opportunity to experience it will reappear in a similar or related form sometime later in life.

Restrictions as metaphors for illness should always be looked upon as an opportunity for personal learning or growth. Most such learning is of a personal, incarnational nature, and often there is little overt outward indication of change as life progresses. Illnesses, once healed, can and do influence those they touch with sometimes dramatic changes in psychology, personality, and lifestyle.

An illness can be secondary to the learning going on. Learning about being dependent or to be cared for by others, is one example. Others learn through nurturing and caring for those who are suffering. This particular growth modality allows two spirits to work together, thus promoting mutual and cooperative spiritual growth. An episode of the original *Kung Fu* television series explored this particular type of learning. The character Caine eloquently expressed it at the end of the episode when he said, "Serving and being served—two sides of the same cloth."

There are instances when the whole point of the learning lesson is contained in the illness experience itself. Depending on the importance of the learning involved, the limitations caused by the illnesses may exist for a short time, or they may last years or perhaps an entire lifetime. When this is the case, there is absolutely no escape from the restriction until the lesson is accepted and experienced. Such uncompromising restrictions may include death itself as a part of the plan. It all depends on the learning needs of the individual and the incarnational life plan in play at the moment.

Learning can be optional or of a less important nature. In these cases, relatively benign illness or restriction is simply a way of saying that things really ought to be changed, but the individual has the choice whether or not to make them. Other times the life of the individual is so far off-track, or the learning is so critically important that the illness cannot be ignored. Events of this nature are termed grounding experiences, a mechanism used to bring attention and focus back to one's self and incarnational priorities, gently or otherwise.

GROUNDING EXPERIENCES

Most of us have designed safeguards into our incarnational plan to ensure that we keep our lives on track. Serendipity and synchroneity often play a role in this process, but backup systems embedded in our physical bodies provide an absolute, failsafe means for grounding and resetting our approach to life if necessary. Most of these come under the category of physical, mental, or medical "predispositions," and are not usually activated unless specifically needed.

Grounding experiences are often benign, showing up with such symptoms as being "run down," or you may simply "crash," sometimes with a cold or flu. Other groundings are more difficult to live through and might include serious illness, injury, or other conditions such as chronic pain.

When learning is critically important, serious illness is often "programmed" into the incarnational plan as a genetic predisposition. When the learning is on track, and the illness is not needed, it isn't activated. Indeed, when your learning and life experiences are both on track, illnesses are not only unneeded, they would be detrimental to the spiritual growth were they to activate.

From the metaphysical perspective, illness is first and foremost a tool for learning. It is not a curse, for learning takes place both when we are "well" and when we are "sick." That there is often pain involved with learning, there is no doubt. Pain is primarily fostered by fear as accentuated by our resistance to accept and immerse ourselves in the lesson at hand. It is important, as a healer, to recognize that fear is not real. Fear is simply a defense raised by the rational mind, a resistance to change, and it often responds well to Reiki or other forms of energy healing.

97

HEALING AS A CHANGE OF DIRECTION

Conventionally we think of sickness as having three phases, that of getting worse, being at the crisis point, and finally recovering and getting back to normal. The crisis point is a term left over from the days of influenza epidemics in the late 1800s and early 1900s when they were pandemic and a serious threat to life. The crisis point signifies the peak of the infection where the patient either started recovery or died. The old adage about the common cold nicely illustrates this perspective in less dramatic terms as "three days coming, three days here, and three days going."

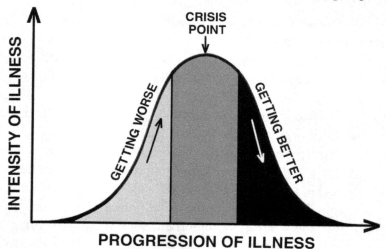

Drawing 4-1 An illustration showing the progression of any sickness where it is described in three phases as getting worse, the crisis interval, and the healing interval.

When Reiki or other healing practices are applied before the crisis point and are successful, they move the progression of illness along the path towards the right. If it happens that the illness is at the beginning stage and the applied healing isn't "strong enough" to move it past the crisis point, the intensity of the illness actually increases the suffering and fosters the perception that the healing failed and only made matters worse. This obviously isn't the case as the healing effort probably shortened the overall length of time that the illness persists, but it is still a disappointment.

When healers decide to offer a healing, the intent should be to move the progression of the illness as far to the right on the curve as possible, hopefully bypassing the need for the sufferer to experience the crisis point. This doesn't always happen, and during the interview process, it is always appropriate to describe the possibility that the result may not be what is expected—the client can actually feel worse following treatment if the crisis point is not passed over.

Both healers and the sufferers who come to them must be prepared to accept that a full recovery is not always possible. It is the duty of the healer to help sufferers accept the results of healing energy that they receive as personally appropriate, regardless of its apparent progress—or lack of it—toward their eventual release from the affliction.

Healing as a Change in Life

The preceding description fits well for illnesses expressed as sickness, but another illustration shows the general view of the healing process when it is considered a restriction controlling a learning or growth experience.

In Drawing 4-2 we show that recovery from illness, rather than sickness, follows the same general course of healing as shown in Drawing 4-1, but now the three phases are renamed as shown.

Once again, illness is a general human condition where restrictions or obstacles in life that, once overcome, result in learning. Sickness is a special case of illness, one that creates a restriction through any combination of mental, emotional, or physical medical infirmities. Illness should never be viewed as a clinical state. Rather, it should be viewed as an opportunity for change to enter one's life, as a sign requesting spiritual growth. The progression of all illness or growth cycles, regardless of their particular manifestation, follows the same three phases from onset to recovery described earlier.

The first phase of a restriction in the general sense, *Discovery and Change*, is the result of some earlier change of direction, perhaps represented by starting a new job or moving into a new apartment. This phase is dominated by the exploration and learning of the new environment. At work you learn the new roles you are to play, or in the new apartment, you try different furniture arrangements and where your kitchen utensils are stored.

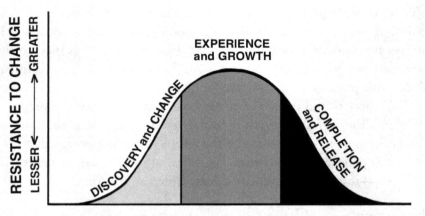

PERIODS IN A TYPICAL LEARNING EXPERIENCE

Drawing 4-2 Healing as a growth experience. Here we see the progression of any aspect of life using essentially the same three phases as that of an illness.

The second phase, *Experience and Growth*, follows as your talents and abilities are applied and developed at work as you learn all there is to know about the job. At home, you've settled in and learn to live comfortably with the neighbors, fix the water heater, and figure out how to make the toilet work more smoothly.

During this phase, there is little motivation to change jobs or your apartment because you still find the job exciting and the apartment is just great. But as time goes on and you move deeper into this phase, the challenges at work become more routine, and you start thinking about how a few changes here and there in the apartment might make the place better.

The third phase, *Completion and Release*, starts as you begin to discover limitations in your present environment. At work perhaps you aren't allowed to implement new processes that you'd like to try, or you might not be allowed to take on new responsibilities that you'd find personally challenging and rewarding. Your apartment starts to feel cramped as you think about expanding your hobbies or family. This is the time when you first start thinking about finding a new, more ideal place to work or live.

As time goes by, dissatisfaction with your job or apartment builds. Eventually, motivation and the willingness begin anew to coalesce as a new direction in life approaches, first as a possibility, then as a probability. The equivalent of the crisis point is reached when the motivation for change meets the end of a completion phase, ideally at the same time.

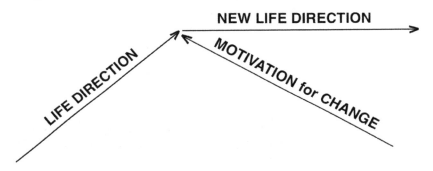

Drawing 4-3 The idealized timing for a life learning lesson. As the experience completes, the motivation for change arrives at which point life branches out in a new direction.

TIMING

Ideally, motivation for change arrives just as a given direction is completed, as shown in Drawing 4-3. But in the real world, personality affects the timing of any change we are willing to make. It is usually the case that we stay in the present direction longer than we should because it is known, safe, and comfortable.

When the motivation for change arrives early or change to a new direction is suppressed, you can become stuck in a rut. No matter how comfortable and safe a rut is, little if any learning takes place there.

Conversely, if an early change is forced, such as jumping into a new job that is beyond your abilities at the time, the result is substantial pain because the uncompleted learning from the earlier direction must still be finished.

But when motivation arrives at just the right time, it feeds the energy and courage needed to make necessary changes. Instead of being a chore

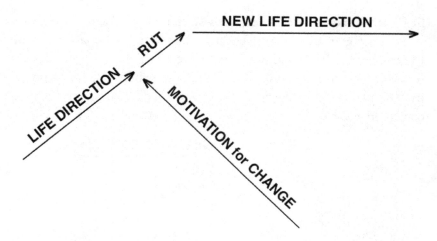

Drawing 4-4 When the energy for change arrives before one is willing to make a change, life turns into a rut. Once that willingness to change arrives, life proceeds in a new and exciting direction.

or an onerous task, the search for the new job or apartment becomes interesting and fun. A firm sense that you've taken the old job as far as it will go, or the realization that the old apartment just isn't big enough, makes the transition to the next direction, the new job or move to the new apartment, smooth and comfortable.

As your life takes on the new direction, the process starts afresh. As an overall principle or algorithm, this is the outline approach for growth and discovery that is found in every aspect of life. From growing out of childhood and into adult life to the general flow from birth to blossoming to death, the pattern, the principle, is apparent and real. This as an unassailable part of nature and of our very essence. It is the flow of creation.

It is no small coincidence that both illness and sickness are responsive to healing energy. Both are, in the final analysis, about spiritual growth whose principal purpose is increased awareness of self. The advanced healer should always be aware that sickness may be but a small part of the overall needs of the sufferer and be ready to supply healing insight to specific needs outside the body as well.

HEALING THE HEALER

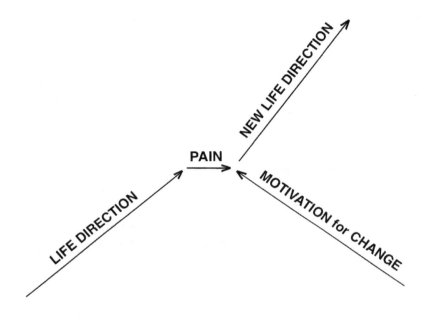

Drawing 4-5 When a new direction in life is taken too early, pain and tension are the results until the motivation for change arrives, at which time, the pain is released and the life proceeds according to the incarnational plan.

Healing others has as much to do with personal validation and growth of healers as it does for those being healed. As healers, we experience the same game as everyone else, with our own learning lessons and baggage to sort through. The only distinction between the healer and sufferer is the role being played.

Experiencing success and failure as a healer is just one of the many mechanisms teaching the lessons we came to learn. Being a healer is not significantly different, from the metaphysical perspective of self, from being a truck driver, a farmer or a politician. Our spiritual stipulation, regardless of the roles we play in society and life, is one of *learning about ourselves*.

It is important that healers do not take on personal responsibility for healing successes or failures. We must understand that the misery that comes before us is not our responsibility. Nor is the outcome of our healing efforts. The entire responsibility for healing lies not with us the healer, but rather with those who come to us, for it is they who wish to be healed. And it is our choice and *never a responsibility* whether or not we choose to serve as the agent of healing for them.

It is the *experience* brought on as life unfolds that benefits both the healer and those asking for help. Being a healer as a way to improve the lives of others is a life choice that we make in our effort to grow and to discover who we are. We should never assume guilt, sorrow or shame for not achieving a 100% record of success, or to become personally affected by the conditions of those coming to us.

Although such feelings are sometimes said to be a part of being human, we must also understand that they reflect the basis for our perspective on life. As such, we have the right and the responsibility to use them as instruments of learning about ourselves, just as we have the responsibility not to allow them to damage or rule our lives.

When we allow thoughts about why a healing did not take place as desired, or when we decide that a failure was in some way our responsibility, we are taking on self-criticism. Self-criticism is never appropriate and reflects that we are not dealing with reality. Rather, we are dealing with a by-product of our rational mind, the thinking that we are in some way inadequate.

When we view a supposed failure to heal, or to help another in some other way, as our fault, it is our rational mind telling us that we should have been able to heal. From there, it tells us, that since we didn't, we are weak and ineffective. Beware of the mind; once again, it is not our friend.

Healing is not a magical process. It is, like everything in creation, an effect following a cause. The physical manifestation of healing is but an optional effect that, when beneficial to the sufferer at some level, may take place.

There are many, many outside influences that can prevent a healing regardless of the healer's experience or "strength." The healing may be incarnationally disallowed, the body has advanced to the stage that it cannot physically recover, or that the client really doesn't want to be healed. All of these and other factors are beyond any healer to overcome.

We are not powerless to control our own feelings and thoughts of inadequacy. When difficulties resulting in stress enters your life, and such thoughts cross your mind, bring reality back into focus by simply asking your body these five questions by reading them aloud:

1) What is it that I see?
2) What is it that I smell?
3) What is it that I taste?
4) What is it that I hear?
5) What physical sensations do I feel?

You must *voice* these questions out loud because your body cannot sense your thoughts. When you wish to communicate with your body, it must be done in some physical manner such as writing (not typing) or speaking, even if in whispers, whatever you'd like to tell it. Your body responds through gut feelings, not thought.

If your thoughts are *interpretive* of these feelings, that is your conscious response. But if your thoughts are just "business as usual thoughts," you are still dealing with your head, not the reality expressed by your body.

By rapidly stepping through the list several times, thoughts of failure, self-criticism, fear, worry or attack on self or others soon dissolve. In practice, do not "concentrate" on receiving an answer. As soon as one appears in the form of unanalyzed feeling or an interpretation of the feeling, immediately and without thought, go to the next question.

If an answer doesn't appear within two or three seconds after the question is asked, immediately go to the next question. If you wait longer for the answer, your rational mind will generate the answer it would like to hear, not the valid response from your body. As the answers flow in, they quickly reset you back inside the bounds of "I am" and "it is."

This simple grounding technique firmly centers you in the moment and stops your mind in its tracks. When you are in the moment, there is no thought. There is only a blissful silence as you realize, without thought, that everything not directly in front of you is harmlessly either in the past or a projection into the uncharted future.

It is only in the moment that you can actually experience experience. And it is only in the moment that you belong as a healer, for it is here that you will do your best work.

HEALING AND SPIRITUAL LAW

Were it not for spiritual law, chaos would rule the physical world and healing of any kind would be impossible. As far as healers are concerned, there are only two spiritual laws that relate to us, both of which are embedded in basic healer philosophy.

These laws are:

1. No spirit is allowed to interfere with the free will of another.
2. No spirit is allowed to impose a debt onto another.

These laws apply to all consciousnesses throughout creation. The first law is plain but specific when it associates the non-interference principle with will. While it may sound like it permits anyone to do anything without regard to the rights of others, this isn't the case. Rather, it is a powerful principle that actually prevents such action by precluding others from arbitrarily imposing on you without your explicit permission. This is the reason that healers must always ask permission to perform a healing.

The term *will* as used here is a nonphysical term. In the nonphysical world, of consciousness and potential, free will is a mandate, and any interference with it amounts to slavery. It is only in the nonphysical realm that we can actually experience *free will*. In the physical world, the nearest equivalent we have to free will is free choice. Because we, living as human consciousnesses, are constrained to experience only particular facets of life at any one time, life is fed to us on the basis of needed learning lessons and our ability to handle the experience.

Although we are never expected to take on something that we are not ready for, we are continuously fed optional experiences related to our core learning. As we choose from them without impediment, we experience free choice.

In the physical, the first spiritual law changes to *"We are not allowed to interfere with the free choice of another."*

The first spiritual law also applies to our efforts as healers. For example, Reiki philosophy stipulates that permission is required before starting treatment. Permission involves two levels of consciousness. The first, the waking conscious (or psychological) level, is where we ask face-to-face for permission: "May I heal you?"

This question is answered implicitly when someone comes to you for a healing. The typical answer is yes, but for a variety of reasons, the real answer, which comes from another level of consciousness, may be no. At the higher level, we are dealing with human courtesy and privacy. After all, a person has the right to be sick and recover on their own without our help. But even when a positive response is given, the person may be less than truthful, for many actually enjoy the benefits of being sick, *i.e.,* the special attention or release from personal responsibility that it brings into their lives.

Be that as it may, the ultimate the permission that we need is given by the actual level of consciousness where the healing is to take place. It is at these (usually) subconscious levels that the particular learning is being accomplished or has been programmed as a part of the incarnational plan. Without clear permission at this level, no root cause healing can take place, regardless of what the sufferer requests or says.

This is not to say that levels of consciousness not immediately associated with the illness waste healing energy when it is refused. Unused or unusable healing energy usually finds some level of consciousness that will accept and use it. Indeed, many psychological benefits are nearly always noticeable following a treatment. This is reflected, for example, in the way that Reiki brings on relaxation and, at least for a time, relieves stress and anxiety on the part of the sufferer. In the hospice setting, Reiki therapy works other miracles by bringing acceptance of the condition and a relaxed, often loving, closure to lives where a physical cure is not possible or appropriate.

The second spiritual law also has relevance for our healing practice. Rephrased in the healing context, it becomes *you are not allowed to perform a healing for someone who has not requested it with an expectation that they will repay you.* This is not the same as taking an "IOU" for a payment.

If you want to arbitrarily perform a healing, you must do it without an agenda. Permission still must have been granted, but you must do it through personal motivation because it pleases you in some way. In other words, in the absence of a payment, the pleasure it brings to you must serve as the payment in its entirety. It is a violation of this law if you perform a healing that wasn't requested because you think it will please someone else as a motivation. Under these conditions, it is a violation of this law for you to expect anything, even thanks, in return.

Unstated expectations are thus spiritually unsound. Reiki philosophy solves this problem with its tradition that we must be paid something for performing a healing.

The effects resulting from violation of the second spiritual law are easily illustrated. Suppose your best friend's family plans a visit. The day before they are to arrive you decide to buy a present for each of the children, thinking that they will be surprised and that you'll get a chance to see them play. But when the day comes, they don't like the presents, and the toys are tossed aside.

A reaction of dismay and disappointment is understandable. You spent your time and no small amount of money on the presents and didn't even get a "thank you." This is the price you pay for violation of the second spiritual law. Nobody asked for the presents, and you gave them with an agenda, an expectation of something in return that wasn't given. The energy you spent on this project was wasted, and that is the loss being felt.

Should there be a request for a healing, the healer may initiate a healing treatment or not, depending on whether or not the healer feels like it. The healer is under no obligation to offer a healing for any reason. The client may not, again under spiritual law, obligate a healing from the healer.

REQUIREMENTS FOR A METAPHYSICAL HEALING

We've discussed a number of topics, and now it is time to put them together to reveal the overall requirements before a nonphysical healing can be manifest.

There are three main requirements. First and foremost, the receiver of the healing must ask for the healing. As just described, this usually comes in at the fully conscious level and is usually the top-level consciousness expressing permission to perform the healing.

But this isn't always the case. At some point, you as a healer may be called on to perform Reiki on an unconscious person, the cause being anything from a motorcycle accident to an advanced form of brain cancer. In cases like this, it is appropriate to offer your healing energy with the intent that it be accepted at some or any level. If you can sense the flow, you'll know right away whether it is being accepted by the client.

Besides granting permission to perform the healing, this question allows the sufferer to describe exactly what is wanted so that the healer's intent can be aligned with the request. Internally, it also represents an opportunity for the sufferer to confront and accept the illness as it is, and thus encapsulate the learning lesson with the healing insight about to be received, making the healing more effective.

If the request is simply something like "make me feel better" the healer should gently help the sufferer focus more on the root cause of the problem and rephrase the appeal. Such a request is simply a denial of the core issues involved. Requests should always in some way express a desire for the source of the affliction to be healed. Without leading, advanced healers always ask for the request to be rephrased (if possible) until it uncovers the real source of the problem.

Extracting the real healing request from first-time clients may take some time. Caring patience in this process is often required as most sufferers asking for a healing never view illness or themselves at this level.

It is at times beneficial to ask the sufferer, after the treatment, to examine the learning being accomplished through the illness. Discussion along these lines often helps the sufferer discover the forces behind the illness, and with that, self-actuated healing will often work alongside the Reiki treatment as it proceeds. Two sources of healing working in tandem are always better than one.

The second requirement is that the sufferer must agree to accept healing offered during the treatment specifically at all levels. This is an agreement at the psychological level, but unfortunately, does not always reflect the situation at lower levels of consciousness. The purpose of this agreement is to help the sufferer align personal healing intent by expressing a willingness to accept change, reinforcing the healing effect initiated by the permission given earlier.

The third requirement is that the requested healing must be appropriate for the sufferer before it can take effect. This is an often overlooked factor when asking why a healing didn't happen. When the life plan is to live through illness, or when a grounding experience is in process but not nearing completion, a healing would actually be a step backward. Although a direct healing in such cases is rejected by the body, the insight gained from the healing effort will further the learning stemming from the grounding experience.

Although it takes substantial experience for healers to develop an intuitive sense about such matters during the interview stage of a healing session, flow sensitivity is generally discovered early on. When flow doesn't "feel right" it represents a resistance to the healing. This can easily be sensed by the healer if attention is continually focused on how the energy flow is behaving during the healing session. It is always appropriate to tell the sufferer when such a resistance is being felt and to ask for help in opening up to the flow.

When this isn't sufficient, advanced healers have the option of going directly to the sufferer's higher self or power for additional help, cooperation, or insight. These sources are the ultimate word on whether a healing is beneficial, incarnationally appropriate, or even possible. The principles and methodology of this approach, alas, must wait for later discussion.

Whenever the sufferer's body rejects the healing energy at the requested level, that energy is often reflected back to the healer. It can also be absorbed by another consciousness level in the client's body that can use it to further promote the learning provided by the illness. Only rarely is healing energy completely rejected, allowing it to pass through the body, unused and wasted.

The only responsibility of the healer is to present the healing energy to be absorbed by the sufferer at some level. It is not the healer's responsibility that the energy be absorbed.

DISCOVERING METAPHYSICAL ILLNESSES

It is possible to sense an oncoming, metaphysically inspired illness before your client is aware of it or feels any physical effects from it. Such illnesses are usually based on the client's rejection of new life direction possibilities or a pre-programmed illness that is a part of the incarnational plan. Life-direction-inspired illnesses can be avoided, whereas a pre-programmed illness cannot, as they are a part of the life experience plan. Such plans are immutable, although their timing is somewhat flexible depending on what is currently being experienced.

Metaphysical illness starts in the outer regions of the nonphysical body. They can be scanned, although it takes an experienced Reiki practitioner to consistently find them. This is because of their ethereal nature. They aren't very "dense" and so are very easy to pass over. Start your exploration for these by having your client lay face up on your massage table. Focus your intent on the discovery of any metaphysical activity in the nonphysical body. Start by sensing the height of the outside nonphysical body, starting at about sixteen to twenty-four inches above the body.

Holding your freshened scanning hand vertical at this height, scan by passing it over the entire length of the body in a single pass. If there is a metaphysical medical condition that is developing you'll feel a very mild "lump" in the nonphysical body at the height you are scanning.

Repeat this process several times, each time with your hand a bit lower until you are just above the body. You need to use total concentration and intense focus on the palm of your scanning hand while probing the nonphysical body because otherwise, you may pick up on a chakra if your focus is a bit off.

If you find a "lump" in the nonphysical body explore it for size. Do this by sensing how long and how tall it is. Illnesses just starting are small and farther away from the physical body. They develop slowly, growing in size as they drift closer to the body. The closer to the physical body they are the more physical (and solid) they become and the sooner they will manifest in the physical. And the larger they are, the more serious will be the sickness brought on by this particular illness.

You should always attempt to give Reiki to such lumps. This may help ameliorate or moderate the coming illness even if it is incarnationally mandated. In other cases, Reiki insight may greatly reduce or completely resolve the need for the illness prior to it entering the physical body.

The majority of metaphysical illnesses express themselves by starting to make your client feel rundown or generally out of sorts. This may be accompanied with a bad cold or perhaps the flu. In any event, the sickness is probably enough to stop whatever activity the client is doing and put him down for a few days. In cases like this, Reiki can be helpful and speed recovery.

The more serious metaphysically inspired illnesses can sometimes result in hospitalization and must be treated by conventional medical practice. So far, I have not discovered a way to predict how serious the illness will become prior to it manifesting itself. In the cases of metaphysical illness, Reiki can help bring healing insight to those so infected, but it is powerless in cases of incarnationally inspired illnesses. In these cases, Reiki will give comfort and calm along with insight that will help your client more easily accept and understand the situation, but he will still have to live through it.

Finding metaphysical illnesses as just described is not easy, and in fact, such illnesses are not common.

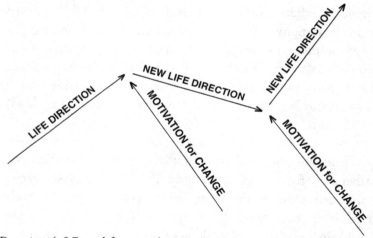

Drawing 4-6 For a life on track, as each restriction is released, life takes on a new and different direction together with a new set of guiding restrictions. This happens as each learning lesson is successfully completed.

We now set out to describe a typical Reiki session. Although the "standardized" positions are no longer stipulated, the client actually receives more healing energy in an hour's session than using the "dogmatic" traditional hand positions. This approach depends entirely on the ability of the healer to detect and feel locations on the body that are willing to accept Reiki energy flow—and those areas that will not. Often times, active areas are located near injuries, but it is common to come across heavy flow in areas not related to them.

Chapter 3, Energy and Consciousness, revealed that energy, including that of a healing nature, is not a consciousness. As such, it has no "intelligence" of its own. The traditional view that Reiki energy is an "intelligent" healing source is a rationalization. It is fostered by the observation that when the desired affliction is not healed, other issues facing the sufferer, such as a mental or nonphysical nature, sometimes receive benefit.

It is an exercise in wishful thinking to state that healing energy "knows what is best for the sufferer." The only entity that knows what is best for the sufferer receiving your healing energy is the spiritual essence of that sufferer. Such knowledge, coupled with the free choice of the sufferer, is the province of the incarnational plan which is not accessible to healers, regardless of persuasion.

There are several factors that generally limit the "strength" of a Reiki treatment. Although Reiki 1 practitioners have received their healing attunement, most Reiki classes do not teach how the Reiki flow can be turned on. Nor do they teach how to sense when the flow is being accepted, or how to find the sensitive locations on the body that will accept heavy flow. And most classes do not teach spiritual law and how it affects a healing session.

How Reiki Works

Reiki and empathic healers are often asked to perform a healing in cases where medical science has failed, or at the least, it has not given the full healing or relief that your client has asked for. We as healers can often give substantive comfort and healing to sufferers where traditional medical treatment has failed, or help when the treatments being given are harsh, such as chemotherapy. Many, if not most, major hospitals now allow the use of volunteer Reiki and other nonphysical healers to visit patients. Patients receiving Reiki generally find comfort and peace in such treatments, even in terminal cases.

The question, "how does Reiki work?" is often asked. The traditional response is that Reiki is smart energy and goes where it needs to go to help satisfy the needs of the client. This appears to be true in many cases—about 30 to 40% of the time. Reiki usually has a calming effect, one that brings peace and tranquility that often helps patients heal as they deal with physical pain and other discomforts

The placebo effect has long been known to be an effective cure for many different conditions. Placebos are pharmacologically inert tablets, drinks, or injections. After examination, the patient is given or prescribed these along with a regimen to follow. Many afflictions, such as colds, asthma, and high blood pressure respond well to placebo treatments. The prescribed use of placebo drugs was generally halted in the US during the 1960s, but today they are often used in "blind" studies of medications under development.

Interestingly, going to a medical doctor and asking for a cure follows the same steps needed for a metaphysical cure. The doctor interviews and examines the sufferer, and then offers a "cure." These steps are also similar to the advanced Reiki healer's approach where, after an interview, Reiki is offered as "the cure."

TURNING ON YOUR HANDS

Reiki healings are based on the interplay of Reiki energy and internal energy systems within the client's body. Healers with only Reiki 1 training perform their healing by touch. Second-degree and Master healers can send Reiki energy without physical touch. Such treatments are usually called distant, or absent, healings where Reiki can be sent to anyone, anywhere, anytime.

Hence it is possible, for example, to send calming Reiki to a meeting taking place sometime in the future, the purpose being to help you and the attendees to relax as you give your presentation.

Reiki cannot give you an unfair advantage over your rivals, but it can help calm you so that you can do your best in whatever situation you're in. It is particularly helpful in high-stress events such as tests, placement exams, personal interviews, or when undergoing medical procedures. The list of high-stress events where Reiki can be of comfort is almost endless.

Freshen your hands (see below), by briefly brushing them on your shirt. Now you can "turn on your hands" by holding them facing each other, maybe three to five inches apart. Wait for the intent to give Reiki to start the flow. The flow will start, perhaps at first somewhat weakly, but because of your intent to give Reiki, it will soon manifest more strongly.

You'll know the flow is present when you "feel something" or simply sense a change in the sensations in your hands. You can verify that the flow is there by moving your hands apart, then back together again. The sensation will fade when your hands are far apart and intensify as they are brought closer together.

Be patient with yourself when you first start trying to feel your Reiki energy. The sensation you are looking for is anything out of your normal hand sensations. It can be a gentle warming, weak "static-like" prickles, a gentle "breeze" or a cooling sensation. In my career, I have only found one student who was unable to sense her own Reiki. Even so, her hands would get very warm, and she'd often break out in a sweat when she gave Reiki.

You can make a "Reiki Ball" by continuing to feed Reiki into the space between your hands. You'll soon find a "resistance" when you move your hands towards each other then apart. With practice—and intent to make a ball—you can easily make a Reiki ball the size of a basketball. With more practice, you can make it big enough to enclose your body. This is an interesting way to perform self-Reiki. Some students find it relaxing to so enshroud their body with Reiki when going to bed at night.

Sensing the flow that is going to a client is much like holding onto a garden hose with the water running. When active, there is a subtle sense sort of like water flowing. The sensation diminishes when the water is turned down, disappearing completely when the water is turned off. This analogy may not be what you sense at all, but it gives you an idea of what to look for.

Another way is to sense the flow with your hands. Re-freshen them, then notice the sensations as you give Reiki. It is almost always the case that your hand sensations will intensify when the flow is active. You can verify the flow by momentarily placing your hands close together, perhaps three to four inches apart. Again, notice the change in hand sensations as your hands approach each other. Eventually, you'll be able to feel the flow with just one hand, your sending hand, but in the meantime, you can get an idea of the strength and flow this way.

FRESHENING YOUR HANDS AND SCANNING

If you quietly turn your focus onto the palms of your hands, you'll find that there are all sorts of sensations being experienced. These consist of prickles, tingling, tickling, warmth and so on. This is background "noise" that can completely mask the energy sensations that you want to sense. Freshening consists of simply brushing your hands on your shirt a couple of times.

This evens out and helps quiet these sensations, making it easier to find a "change" when your hand is passed over an energy center or the feelings in your hands when Reiki flow is present. The sensations vary from one student to the next. They will be subtle, but they will be there.

Almost everyone finds comfort in using either the right or left hand for sensing the energy centers in the client. When first starting out, you'll have to experiment to find which hand is most sensitive or works the best for you. It is the case that almost never are both hands equally sensitive. This also applies when giving Reiki—one hand, usually not the sensing hand, almost always seems more powerful.

To determine which hand is more sensitive, you'll need a patient volunteer to lie face up on your therapy table while you learn to sense the energy coming from the heart chakra, which is usually the most active of the chakras. You probably want to turn off any music and other electronic devices while doing this as they are a distraction, something you don't need when learning to sense the subtle energy fields surrounding the chakras.

Freshen whichever hand you want to start out with and wait while the background sensations settle out, then with your palm facing down and about five inches above your volunteer's chest, move it at a steady rate across the heart area. You'll want to move at a fairly good rate, rather than a slow, methodical speed. This is because you're now looking for a *change* in the sensations you feel in your hand. If you go too slowly, the change won't be as easily found.

The change you'll feel as you cross the chakra is very subtle, so focus on your palm is all important. With a little effort, you should be able to "pick up" on the change. You must be careful to keep your mind quiet while doing this because it'll attempt to tell you that you imagined what you just felt.

After you've worked with your volunteer a little while, try scanning with your other hand. Freshen it, then, after the sensations have quieted down wave it over the heart chakra just as you did with your first hand. You will find that you are able to better pick up on the sensations with one hand or the other. This will be your sensing hand, and in the future, you should use it when scanning.

Your non-scanning hand will typically be better able to send Reiki than your sensing hand although there is no reason not to use both when giving Reiki. Just remember to freshen your hand before attempting to sense the various chakras and other sites you will have an interest in and depending on your client's needs.

NONTRADITIONAL REIKI

It is possible to take advantage of the nonphysical realm when using Reiki. None of what follows should be considered as "the final word." Dealing with the nonphysical aspects of ourselves is tricky when the rational and ever-present mind is at work. For best understanding of what follows you should close your mind and keep it locked up in a cage. Remember that the mind is always correct, even when it is wrong. The mind considers itself to be "perfect" and that is what it would have you believe.

Once you have mastered the art of turning on your hands and to specifically sense body sensations, you are ready to change the traditional dogmatic approach of a healing session to one that is more participatory, one in which no time is wasted attempting to give Reiki to body locations that are not accepting Reiki.

I teach that the traditional hand positions are not "magic" and are used to hopefully, but through accident, give Reiki to a few locations where the flow will be heavy over the course of the session. The non-physical approach goes a step further by stipulating that Reiki should be given only to those locations where there is significant flow rather than spending time on positions where there is no flow.

This means that you should follow your hands rather than "your head" as you give Reiki. Your body scan will locate areas that will conduct heavy Reiki flow, even though they may not be locations normally given Reiki. This is particularly true when treating clients who have suffered injuries. It is usually the case that heavy Reiki flow will occur around and over such injury sites as well as at locations quite removed from them.

In practice, one should conduct a body scan first with the intention of finding emotional issues that are, or soon will be, blocking your client's happiness. Give Reiki at those sites to eliminate these causes before continuing. Next, scan for sources of physical distress and treat them. Finally, give Reiki to sites with heavy flow, *colored* to match the sensations that you sense or by your intent which is hopefully flavored by your intuition rather than by analytical means. Typically emotional and physical sites are in different locations.

Healers with Reiki 2 training can make use of their empowerment and mental symbols during the treatment where specifically strong Reiki flow exists.

The above is the most "pure" form of Reiki treatment, although there is no apparent record of Dr. Usui using a draining or transferring technique which I consider absolutely necessary if you are to do your best work. Nor did he (apparently) teach training the hands to sense the body's needs or scanning. Traditional Reiki treatments are given as a "one-size-fits-all" approach regardless of any special needs on the part of the client.

And so as your experience with your Reiki healing practice increases, it should center on "follow your hands." Now is a good time to expand this to "follow your hands, gut feelings and five senses" for as your mind is throttled back and put under control, you'll be able to better sense all of the subtle energies and sensations around you and your client through one or more of your five senses.

The sensations that you can sense when doing any form of energy healing are only limited by how quiet you can maintain your mind, the natural sensitivity of your physical senses, and your awareness. What your awareness can pick up from your senses and bring to your consciousness is limited by where you place your focus and how narrowly you can bring it to bear.

As human beings, we tend to be quite visual, and since most of us don't see much happening when giving Reiki, it is a common practice to close our eyes in order to remove unwanted sensory input. This is a meditational way of sharpening focus and of removing "noise" from the analytical parts of our consciousness. Logically, this makes sense: if you don't see anything, then there's nothing to see, so why not remove the non-useful input?

There is another way of expressing this. What our mind is telling us is that to see more, we should close our eyes. This logical fallacy presupposes that there isn't anything to see. Visual information, whether the mind "sees" it or not contains many clues about what is happening at any given moment. When you are connected to your client or your healing energy, your mind is not in use. There is only perception—perception without analysis, and your mind doesn't like this!

As a result, you may occasionally witness fields of color as you give your Reiki. Or you may feel activity on your wrists and arms. Some healers pick up odors or hear sounds. It all depends on the individual practitioners, their native talents, abilities and experience level.

With your eyes closed and with experience you can eventually start seeing these "colors" more frequently. They ebb and flow as the Reiki energy passes through you and into the client. With (considerably) more effort, you'll find that you can color this energy, and with your sensitive hands, actually sense the "amount" of flow. This allows you to match your Reiki energy color to meet the needs of the client and get maximum flow.

When healing or doing energy work, what you consciously perceive is entirely dependent on where you place your focus. Your mind is not useful or beneficial when you are giving Reiki or doing other forms of energy work. Focus and being in the moment, when performing a healing, is necessary for best work.

And so as we learn to sense the subtle energy patterns, it is important that you learn to narrow your focus to those senses and areas of your body that you wish to use. Best results will be had with complete detachment from everything else.

It is difficult to teach this particular subject, and so it is mostly up to you, the student, to learn how to move into the moment when doing your healing. The best advice, when you are starting out, is that when you find yourself thinking about anything, then stop it! Beginners find this is far easier said than done, yet this is what must be learned. Shutting off the mind takes a lot of work—it amounts to training your mind to keep quiet.

Most of our physical senses are not commonly employed when healing or sensing energy flow. The narrowing of focus does not mean disregarding most all of your senses. Depending on you, the healer, energy patterns can be sensed visually, through smell and taste, sound, and of course, tactilely through touch.

Although you may not at present have the sensitivity to use all five senses at once, you should nonetheless continually scan through all your senses asking yourself, "What is it that I smell?", "What is it that I feel?", "What is it that I see?", "What is it that I hear?", and lastly, "What is it that I taste?" These questions should be answered without thought. Overall, this practice will help keep you grounded in physical reality and in the moment as it expands your awareness and sensitivity to the subtle energies flowing around you.

Your ultimate personal sensitivity to subtle energy flow is obtained by simply quieting your mind so that its noise no longer masks the feelings evoked by the energy flows you wish to sense. An additional positive influence is learning to tightly focus individually on those areas of your body—such as the palms of your hands—whose sensors you are using. And with practice, you'll be able to also focus on very small patches on your client's body, rather than seeing it all—or a lot of it—at once.

In the final analysis, it is your body's physical sensitivity, a matter that we all have to accommodate, that determines your best sensitivity threshold. Some of us have more sensitive hearing, eyesight, smell, taste and touch thresholds than others, just as some have more athletic ability.

Although it is a matter of genetics that we all are born with that determines how well you can experience subtle energy flows, most people benefit and improve their ability to detect subtle energy flow with dedicated practice. Dedicated practice means setting up a fixed schedule where you close yourself off from the world to meditate or practice your Reiki for at least fifteen minutes to an hour every day.

MAKING AN ENERGY ASSESSMENT

Before the hands are turned on at the beginning of a session, the healer should make an energy assessment of the client prior to starting the actual treatment. This procedure can be performed by anyone with Reiki or empathic training. It will take some experience before you are able to sense the nonphysical body layers, but rest assured that with patient practice you'll eventually be able to do this.

To make an assessment, freshen your sensing hand and begin with your client resting comfortably face up on your therapy table. This protocol consists of the following steps:

Step 1. Find the ovum layer over the heart chakra. In a healthy client, this will generally be sixteen to twenty-four inches in height. You should perform this step over all of the chakras, and between them, including the two in the feet. In a healthy adult body, the ovum will generally be no less than eight inches in height above the body. If significantly lower, this indicates that something, probably unwholesome, is going on. What this "something" is happens to be none of the healer's business; it is just an indication that *somewhere* the body will support and accept heavy energy flow. It is up to you, the healer, to find that location.

Step 2. Check the crown chakra. This may be difficult at first, but it is essential in assessing the client. It will be found anywhere, from three or four inches from the top of the head to perhaps as much as a foot or two away from the head. Freshen your sensing hand as necessary as you go along. A good, strong reading relatively high above the head typically indicates a spiritually strong client, while a closer less energetic value indicates someone who is more physically inclined. A "heavy" or "energetic" sensation at any height generally means that the client is fundamentally healthy.

Step 3. Scan over the body's main chakras. What we are looking for here is that they are all active with none particularly depressed. Some time may need to be spent working with any depressed chakra during the session after the assessment is complete.

Step 4. Continue your body scan until you've passed over the entire body.

We now do a frontal body scan, this time specifically looking for places where there will be a heavy (or heavier than average) Reiki flow. When such a location is found, give it Reiki for two or three minutes, then scan it again to see if it will accept additional Reiki. After the location no longer accepts heavy flow, proceed with the rest of your full body scan.

Once again and in detail, these are the steps that you should use after freshening your sensing hand at the beginning of each step:

Step 1. Set your intent to discover those areas that are receptive of Reiki energy, then, with your sensing hand three or four inches above the body, move your hand above and around the head, all the while looking for places where there is Reiki flow. When you locate an area that will accept heavy flow, give Reiki to that area.

Step 2. Check the face and throat area.

Step 3. Go on to the main part of the body. Since your intent is to locate places where Reiki flow will be strong, this time around you won't be sensing the chakras on these passes unless one or more of them accepts your probing Reiki, or you've lost focus on your hands.

Step 4. Finish by scanning both legs and feet.

Give Reiki to those sites willing to accept flow. At this point, you'll have a good overview of where your Reiki flow was most easily absorbed by the body. Depending on how much time you have left in the session, a second head-to-toe scan on the client's back is often useful, stopping to give Reiki at any location that will draw it. As the session comes to an end, turn the client onto his back and drain the chakras. Note to Reiki 2 practitioners: this should be done even when using absent Reiki.

OPENING AND DRAINING THE CHAKRAS

This part of the healer's practice varies widely from Reiki Master to Reiki Master, but it is an uncomplicated process. This is a part of the healer's art that helps relax a client. Some healers perform a draining at the start of a session in hopes that it will make the body more readily absorb Reiki while others perform draining at the end of the session. There are many ways to "drain chakras." The following empathic approach is one that works well for me:

Step 1. Go to the feet and offer Reiki with the intent that it will open the chakras there. (You can do this to both feet simultaneously, with one hand on each foot.) Once they are opened, go to the hands and open these chakras. And finally, go to the head and in the same manner open the crown chakra. Once it is open, give it Reiki with the intent that Reiki energy will pass through the body, flushing out old, tired energy through the feet and hands and into the earth, replacing it with fresh, clean Reiki energy.

Step 2. Freshen your sensing hand and scan the feet and hands for energy that is leaving the body. If it doesn't feel "strong," give Reiki to the crown chakra for another minute or two, again with the intent that it will flush out the stale energy and replace it with fresh energy.

Step 3. Return to the feet and hands and verify that the flow has increased. Go to the crown chakra and give it additional Reiki. Continue this position for another minute or two (or however long you feel is appropriate) then return to the feet and hands, giving Reiki with the intent of closing off the flow.

Step 4. Leave the crown chakra as it is; it will close of its own accord. Finish the draining exercise by scanning all the chakras. By now they should be fairly strong and for the most part, uniform as sensed by your freshened hand.

NOTES ON THE TRADITIONAL REIKI TREATMENT

Traditional Reiki treatments prescribe that you give Reiki to some of seventeen or more "standardized" locations. In a typical session, about half of them are on the front of the client, with the rest on the back. These positions cover the entire body literally from head to toe. In a typical one-hour session, that means to cover them all you must change hand positions about every three minutes, turning the client over onto the stomach to get the back locations midway through the session.

The typical treatment doesn't include all positions, an impracticality for an hour's session, and so many positions, at the discretion of the healer, are omitted. Reiki is blindly given to areas where there is no flow. Even so, at least some Reiki will be briefly given those locations that will probably accept it, although it is a less than an ideal healing session.

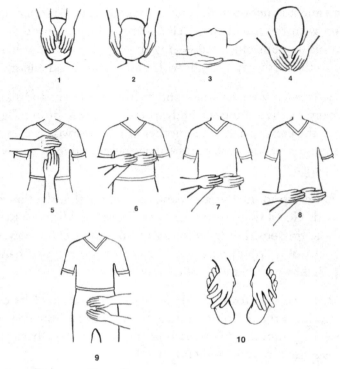

Traditional Front of Body Locations

There are many variations and others taught in Reiki 1 classes; the positions shown are typical.

Position 1: Cover eyes and forehead with fingers alongside the nose.

Position 2: Cover the temples with fingers touching the cheekbones.

Position 3: Back of head resting on hands with fingertips past the skull.

Position 4: Hands covering the front of the neck (avoid touching the throat).

Position 5: One hand covering lower heart, the other over the esophagus-stomach.

Position 6: Both hands above the solar plexus.

Position 7: Both hands over the navel.

Position 8: Both hands over the waist.

Position 9: Both hands over the groin (males) or pubic bone (women).

Position 10: If only treating the front of the body, hands on the bottoms of the feet. Otherwise, skip to Position 11.

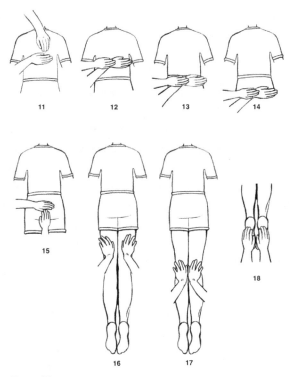

TRADITIONAL BACK POSITIONS
These positions are not used if only working on the front of the body.

Position 11: One hand over the upper spine, the other across the top of the lungs.
Position 12: Both hands just below the shoulder blades.
Position 13: Both hands over the spleen/kidneys.
Position 14: Both hands on upper hips.
Position 15: One hand over the sacrum, the other above the coccyx, forming a "T".
Position 16: Hands over the thighs.
Position 17: Both hands on the back of knees.
Position 18: Hands on the pads of the feet.

The traditional hand positions won't be commented on as there are plenty of books, many of them imitative, which describe these and other positions. The book that I supply as a part of my Reiki 1 classes is *The Power of Reiki: An Ancient Hands-on Healing Technique* by Tanmaya Honervogt, ISBN 0-8050-5559-2. Inexpensive and nicely produced, it is a complete guide for beginning Reiki students and clearly shows all the "standard" positions as well as many variations.

Nearly all Reiki practitioners play soft, relaxing music in the background during the session. The purpose for using background music is first to help the client relax. Second, it helps to reduce the distracting effects of background noise, and finally, it gives the practitioner something to listen to while quietly standing still, arms outstretched, for an hour's session.

The music used typically ranges from "twangy" droning music from India to that of meditative New Age. You can use any music that you feel is helpful. As an example, I use New Age music in a custom program mix that I built up. It always starts with the same "emersion" piece. This signals the repeat client that the session has started and that it is time to chill out and relax. The center piece is a new age selection (or selections) and the third piece, again always the same, slowly wakes the client at the end of the treatment.

Used every time, the beginning and ending musical titles replace verbal direction from the healer that in itself may delay or even prevent total relaxation. One of the best relaxation CDs I have found is *The Silent Path* by Robert Haig Coxon. Music by Steven Halpern, especially his earlier titles, is excellent as well.

CRYSTAL TECHNOLOGY

A lot of information and misinformation about crystals has been published over the years. As you start working with crystals it is important that you understand that your reality is what you see, hear, smell, taste, and feel. If you have none of these sensations at play, then you have no way of understanding what is happening, if anything.

You've probably read or at least heard about "Reiki Crystal Grids" for doing everything from "healing the earth" to curing baldness. Similar such information is often associated with New Age groups espousing things like "pyramid" power, possibly with a direct link to UFOs.

The popular literature is heavy on largely content-free stories and very light on practical use or technique. I have found that most literature on the subject consists of information obviously lifted from other sources. It is a matter of authors wanting to write about something they've only read about, with little or no in-depth, personal understanding of the subject. If there is a definitive work on the subject of crystal use and application, I have yet to find it.

I decided to personally explore whether there was anything to crystal practice, and if so, to see how crystals might be used in conjunction with Reiki to deliver greater potency and efficacy. Much to my surprise, I found many applications for crystal use when performing a healing:

1. Crystals can be used to provide a continuous flow of Reiki (and other) healing energies without requiring your constant participation.

2. Crystals can boost the flow of Reiki that you can provide.

3. Crystals can help "tune" your Reiki energy color for best effect on your client.

4. Crystals can be an additional source of healing energy as you are giving Reiki using your absent Reiki techniques.

The terminology that follows is mine alone, as far as I know. The overall application strategy is what I decided to use, most of which was intuitively set up and tried. Other approaches, if you care to experiment and discover them on your own, may work equally well, and conceivably even better. Crystals are said to work best for their owners, and so your care and companionship of and with them may determine how useful they are to you.

You should consider the following when using crystals:

1. You are the expert on your personal use of crystals and any other healing technique that you make use of. You alone know

what your sensations are reporting, and you alone can interpret them. My experience is that one's sensations, when giving Reiki, are unique to the individual practitioner, although most often there are some general similarities from one practitioner to another. The same applies to crystal use.

2. None of the following instructions are based on *your* reality. Until you can duplicate the various practices that are described, you should consider them as guidelines for experiments that may or may not work for you. After you've tried these approaches and find them to work yourself, then you can consider them "real." And you may find that modification of my approaches or entirely new ones work better for you. There is no right or wrong way to use crystals, just as there is no right or wrong way to give Reiki.

3. Be wary of your mind. After successfully completing an experiment it will soon tell you it was all a joke and didn't work at all, questioning the logic behind your discoveries, even though we already agree there is no logic to it. Remember that gut instincts always tell you what is true before your head (your mind) has figured it out.

4. My experience is that once you've found something that works for you, it will always work for you and can be trusted, just as is your ability to give Reiki. This, despite the objections your mind will throw your way. I have not found "down days" where crystal use, once having been tried and verified, failed to work.

5. Use of crystals, because it is based on your intent, follows the same spiritual laws as does Reiki. Thus crystals cannot cause harm to either you or your client. At worst, they will not work at all, which is a rarity.

Minerals and crystals have a "natural" or "vibration" energy flow coming from them many of which can be sensed. The quartz crystals that are used in my Reiki classes serve as a neutral transmitter, vibration translator, and energy storage capacitor rather than as a primary source of energy. Quartz crystal is a "wideband" crystal that accepts energy in its immediate environment from a wide range of sources and reradiates that energy as if it were its own.

It is possible for quartz crystals, through your intent, to pick up energy from another crystal or mineral source and transfer it to a target, be it a person or animal, a plant or inanimate object, or even another crystal. Your crystals can be used to collect, store and transfer Reiki energy that you supply. That you can do this as a Reiki 1 practitioner is useful, but it will not be until you receive your Second Degree attunements that crystal technology will reach its full potential for you.

Your Crystal Set

Your introduction to crystals needs four (or more) Arkansas AAA Fine quartz crystals. These crystals are sold by the pound ($40) and should be selected to measure about 2-1/2" long when you purchase them. Select one of them, say the largest one, to serve as your "master" crystal. The others have no particular name. I call them "target crystals." (You can also purchase larger more perfect crystals starting at $10–15 each. These are more attractive but are no more effective.)

Before doing anything else, you must spend time to get acquainted with your crystals. Laying them on a plain piece of white paper to separate them from other energy fields on the table, scan them using your standard Reiki scanning procedure to feel their residual energy. Each crystal probably has a different energy "level" or strength, and possibly this energy feels "different" than what you've felt before.

The energy strength and its feel that you perceive is the residual energy held by the crystal. Most of it probably came from those who handled it in the past, although energy from various minerals that have been in its close proximity may be stored in it as well.

Before using your crystals, they must be cleared of this residual energy one by one. First, give the crystal of your choice a couple minutes of Reiki, then with your intent for the crystal to release all of its stored energy, touch it to something heavy such as a small rock. If this is inconvenient, use running water and the drain in your kitchen sink. After doing this, dry it and use your freshened sensing hand to see that there is no residual energy left in the crystal. Your intent to discharge the crystals is all-important.

As an aside, before use of crystals, it is a common practice to "cleanse" them. There is no definitive source detailing why or specifically how this is best done, and nothing but anecdotal stories about why we should bother with the practice are to be found.

Cleansing techniques vary across the board from packing your crystals in "sea salt" to baking them in the sun to some really strange rituals in moonlight. Given that it is easy to do, we will cleanse them by simply washing them in plain running tap water in a convenient sink as just described. This is to be done immediately after "discharging" them and needs to be done only once unless later on they've been handled by someone besides yourself. After carefully drying your crystals, they are ready for use.

STORING YOUR CRYSTALS

Many advocates indicate that your healing crystal set should be kept as near you as much of the time as possible because it is said, they will "pick up and store your identity, capturing the energy field surrounding you." This supposedly makes them specifically "attuned" to your intent and capabilities. I have experimented with this and have found no evidence to support these claims in my particular case.

That your crystals are part of your "medicine kit" makes them very personal tools. But their use, as will be described shortly, is to move your intent, not "store your identity" or other energy remnants that you may impart to them. (The first step in using them is to discharge anything stored in them, and so there would go your stored identity in any event.) They are not pets, they are tools.

Having said that, in general, it is best to not allow others to handle your crystals. If they do and you feel strongly about this, discharge them once again, cleanse them, then recharge them and leave them near you for a few days. That should get rid of all the "evil spirits" that they've picked up.

Treat your crystals with respect, as they are fine tools. I recommend making a special box for them to be stored. I lined my box (a wooden cigar box) with blue velvet fabric with a segmented compartment for each crystal.

CHARGING YOUR MASTER CRYSTAL

Quartz crystals can be energized or charged under any light conditions. The charging energy that you'll use is entirely intent-based and starts with your master crystal. Select one to be used as your master crystal and set aside the others for the moment. Lay it on the plain piece of white paper in front of you, start your Reiki flow, and place your hands over the crystal for a few moments, perhaps two or three minutes (or more if you wish).

Remove your hands, stop your Reiki flow, then scan the crystal with your freshened sensing hand and feel the energy coming from it. Give additional Reiki to the crystal and re-scan, noticing that the energy level is at least somewhat higher than before.

Discharge the crystal, and repeat the exercise several times to gain familiarity and the feel of your particular crystal. Once you feel comfortable with this process, charge your master crystal by giving it additional Reiki and temporarily set it aside on the paper.

The energy that you just felt coming from your master crystal is your natural "frequency" or "vibration" value. Everyone has an individual natural frequency ranging from very physical to highly mental. That is why some healers do better on physical healings, and others are seen to operate best on mental or spiritually endowed clients. It is difficult to "tune" your natural frequency to match the best needs of your client without the use of crystals, although with much practice and effort it can be done during a typical Reiki session.

Quartz crystal has the ability to change your natural frequency to another, virtually without loss. It is, therefore, important, as an advanced healer, for you to be able to recognize the different feelings of energy that is best suited for your client as evidenced by the flow intensity and color. This effect also takes place when using your master crystal to charge target crystals.

Charging Target Crystals

Leaving your master crystal charged, place one of your other crystals on the paper. This is your "target" crystal, one that we will charge from your master crystal in just a moment. Scan the target crystal and if necessary discharge and cleanse it. Re-scan it once again to ensure that it is fully discharged, discharging it yet again if you feel it necessary.

Once the target crystal is fully discharged, set it down on the paper. Pick up your master crystal and touch it to the target for a second or two with the intent that the target should be charged with the same energy as the master crystal. Lay the master crystal back down on the paper, away from the target and scan both the target and the master crystal for identical energy intensity and feeling.

When you have mastered this process, the result will be that the master crystal retains its full charge and the target has received the same charge. Practice discharging the target and recharging it until you have this procedure down. Be sure to check your master crystal, adding Reiki to it as needed to keep its charge at a fairly high level.

As an exercise, you can extend this experiment by charging a second target crystal using either the master or the newly charged first target crystal. Keep working at it in this manner until you can charge all of your target crystals, either all of them from the master or one by one from each other.

Transferring Charge From Crystal to Crystal

This experiment is conducted just like before except now we transfer all the charge from the master crystal to the target, leaving the master crystal discharged. The only thing that changes is your intent. Perform this experiment several times until you can successfully transfer all the charge from the master crystal to the target on the first try, then all of the charge from the first target crystal to the second, and from the second to the third, and finally, from the third target back to the master.

You should note the striking similarity between transferring charge from crystal to crystal and our draining exercises. This technique is also essentially the same as healing by transference, an empathic approach.

TRANSFERRING CHARGE FROM CRYSTAL TO WATER

This experiment may take some time for you to master, but it is one that you should work on until you have it down. We start with a glass of freshly drawn tap water in a glass or a bottle of water. Scan the water for signs of residual energy, discharging any that you find. You may find that whether your glass is made of glass or plastic makes a difference in your early perception of this energy, but in time and with lots of practice it won't make much difference. But for now, use whichever type of container works best, then practice with the "troublesome" type of container sometime later. Eventually, for convenience, you'll want to practice using bottled water, or you can start using it now. It's your choice.

Start your Reiki flow and give the glass (or bottle) of water Reiki for a short period of time, say thirty seconds to a minute. Scan the glass for energy. Repeat as necessary until you can clearly sense the energy stored in the water by passing your freshened sensing hand over it. If you have difficulty in storing energy in the glass of water, take out your master crystal and give it two or three minutes of Reiki, then touch it to the water container with the intent that it should receive the stored energy in your crystal.

You should now easily be able to verify that the glass of water has Reiki energy in it. If you had difficulty charging the glass of water directly from your hands, this use of your quartz master crystal demonstrates how it can "translate" or shift your natural frequency to that of the target—the glass of water—when direct Reiki fails.

Ordinarily, you will charge water for a specific purpose with some definite intent, then consume it, apply to the body as a part of a skin lotion, or use it to water plants or give in some way as a Reiki treatment. Or it can also simply be disposed of. For now, you need to practice, and so you can discharge the glass of water just as you do crystal energy and start again.

Those who have taken Reiki 2 can use crystals to make a "Reiki Machine" a device you can set up with your crystals to give Reiki absent healings on a round-the-clock basis. Details explaining how to set up such a device are given in Chapter 5.

HEALING ELIXIRS

Once you have charged your glass of water, you've created the base for what is commonly called an "elixir." You can store elixirs if you start with tap, spring, or bottled water. Elixirs should be stored in a tightly sealed, clean or sterilized container. You can also make and store the elixir in an "uncharged form" in a bottle then charge it specifically for each use.

You can also use quality liqueurs and hand lotions as your elixir base. Elixirs are useful and ideal for chronic conditions because they can store and retain your healing intent and be dispensed by your client as needed over a period of time. Your intent and healing are released when taken directly from time to time or applied in lotion form directly to the skin over affected areas being treated.

For many new clients, it is a stretch just to accept a "normal" Reiki treatment. Explanations or details of how elixirs are made and how they work as treatment methodologies are not appropriate in most cases. If you feel that the client would benefit from an elixir, the fact that you've been asked to perform a healing by the client is your permission to offer it, the same as your Reiki. But you are never under an obligation to reveal how Reiki or your elixirs work.

I give a Reiki-infused bottle of water to clients at the end of each session. Drinking water after any Reiki therapy session is always appropriate. Giving your client an elixir—even though the base is just bottled water that has been given Reiki—is within normal treatment bounds.

In any event, when your elixir is consumed, the effect is twofold. First, the Reiki energy plus that given by you or by way of your crystals used to make the elixir is directly absorbed into the body. Second, the water in the elixir transports residual toxins resulting from the healing to the bladder where they are expelled in due course.

Caution: An extreme contraindication for giving alcohol-based elixirs is warranted if your client has, or ever has had, an addiction to alcohol. If this is the case, no alcohol in any amount or in any form should ever be offered. Stick to bottled water—that is the safest elixir base to use.

If your client suffers from an alcohol issue, you can safely use a water-based elixir or bottled water. In fact, you can charge up nearly anything that can be consumed, and it is especially good if it has a high water content. Many Reiki Masters make it a habit of doing Reiki on their food and beverages at every meal. In any event, Reiki applied to anything eaten will carry the same effect to your client as an elixir, but typically does not carry the same charge potency.

Applications for your elixirs do not need to stop here. They can be used on animals and plants as well. Plants, in particular, tend to respond well to Reiki and Reiki-enhanced fertilizers. Several student papers showing this have been published.

CRYSTAL ELIXIRS

We stipulate that common crystal or mineral practice prepares elixirs by soaking them in water, although most texts seem to avoid giving specific recipes or procedures to be followed. The following is for reference only.

For typical crystal-based elixirs, a crystal or mineral sample is selected for its appropriate energy for the problem (health or otherwise) being worked on and soaked in the elixir base fluid (usually plain tap water) for several hours or days. The elixir can be used immediately or capped for later use.

The distinction between Reiki and ordinary crystal elixirs is not so much in their preparation but as to how they are formulated as a healing agent. Reiki energy is supplied to the elixir base only as an intent to heal and is given without thought, diagnosis of a problem or any other analysis. Crystal and herbal energy (and by that we mean the particular crystal types or herbs to be used) must be selected according to the diagnosed illness to have the best possible effect.

There are some published notions that depending on the particular crystal elixir being concocted that some should be prepared in bright sunshine and others in moonlight. Crystal elixirs are often said by such sources to be best stored under a "pyramid" shape and perhaps surrounded by protective crystals. I have found no benefit from any of these practices.

It is clear that practitioners using only crystal and herbal cures demand use of a substantial knowledge base and a large crystal/mineral selection as well as herbs. Few such practitioners can intuitively understand the necessary energies available from such natural sources to effect a particular cure. Given the dogmatic nature of such literature, it is apparent that little original thought, effort, or depth of understanding stands behind most of these texts.

The main distinction between crystal and conventional medicine is that crystal remedies, being "energy" in nature, hopefully, work on non-physical bodies, thus encouraging a reflective cure into the physical. A good part—if not all—of ordinary crystal healing is probably due to just the placebo effect.

In my experience, Reiki energy and treatment is not affected by concerns such as lighting conditions or what direction the client is facing during a crystal treatment. However, for Reiki 2 students, informed studies on the effects Reiki treatments using elixirs would make for marvelous and original papers.

CHAPTER 5

REIKI AND MINERAL MACHINES

When we say that we understand a group of natural phenomena, we mean that we have found a constructive theory that embraces them.
—Albert Einstein

This chapter gives advanced crystal techniques and absent healing protocols for those who have received their Reiki 2 attunements. Those of you with only Reiki 1 experience will find the following interesting, but not available until you've taken a Reiki 2 class and have received the attunements.

So from this point forward, we'll assume that you've taken your Reiki 2 course and have noticed the remarkable increase in power as you work in your healing-by-touch sessions. We will also assume that you feel comfortable and proficient in this practice. And by now you should have access to a full-sized massage therapy table. It will make giving Reiki far easier, and your clients will be much more comfortable during the sessions. There is no other practical alternative.

The following describes a "hands-on" treatment. Notice the difference in this approach compared to a traditional Reiki session.

WATCHING THE FLOW

It is possible to observe (but not "see" with your eyes) the energy flow of Reiki as it reaches your client and disperses throughout the body. Such observation best takes place after you've reached a calm, meditative state and with your eyes closed. This observation can take place using either hands-on or absent Reiki protocols.

For best work, your treatment room should be quiet or equipped with quiet, meditative music of your choice and a silent (no ticking) clock to keep track of your healing sessions.

Before starting the treatment explain to any guest accompanying your client the need for quiet; you will be entering a meditative zone, and noise of any kind or from any source is disruptive. You should offer your client a pillow and blanket if that will help them feel more comfortable. Ideally, your client should go to sleep during the session.

Once on the table, there should be minimal verbal discourse with your client or guests if you allow them in the treatment room. Some Reiki practitioners don't allow them during the treatment session. It must be admitted that even with the guests being quiet as a mouse, they still are a distraction. As a general rule, I don't allow accompanying visitors in the treatment room during the session unless I am treating children when an accompanying adult presence is mandatory. Their attendance serves primarily to give comfort to the child as well as to prevent possible legal issues.

The restrooms should be visited by both the client and guest and any reading material for the guests should be in hand prior to the start of the session. Busy out the telephone and turn off all cell phones. You're looking for quiet here. Check the time on your clock, which should be easily visible from where you'll be working, then begin your chill-down after starting the background music. I remove rings and wrist watches and ask clients to do the same as these can become distractions as well.

I start my treatments by giving hands-on Reiki to the solar plexus and crown chakras for two or three minutes with eyes closed. When the flow slows down, I place the power symbol (Cho-Ku-Rei) on the solar plexus chakra. This practice particularly helps the client quickly settle down and more easily close his eyes for greater relaxation. (Out of respect to traditional Reiki provisions, no pictorial images of the Reiki symbols will be given in what follows.)

Next, the chakras are drained as described in Chapter 4. Now a full body scan is performed, again as described in Chapter 4, but with the intent to locate emotional sites on the body that will accept heavier Reiki flow. By giving Reiki to the client at these strategic locations at the beginning of the session, further relaxation is provided. This step is skipped if no mental locations are found.

At these locations you may be able to start perceiving the color of the flow, provided you keep your eyes closed and your mind quiet. The flows have little form, but the colors I typically observe are orange, green, or a bluish-white, usually not mixed. Other colors show up from time to time. Color observation is entirely dependent on the practitioner and the flow. They aren't "visual," meaning they aren't something your eyes can perceive, and they don't always show in the same color discovered in previous sessions.

When we say you can "perceive" the flow of Reiki, we do not mean that you can see it with your eyes. In fact, your eyes should, for the most part, be closed throughout the session to block out distraction that would otherwise pull you out of your meditative state. The flow that you most probably will sense will be like flowing clouds of one predominant color or another in your mind's eye.

Such fields of color have little or no form, just shades of color. When the flow is heavier the clouds become somewhat more distinct. And as the flow diminishes the clouds and color also diminish in form and texture until there are no color or flowing shapes remaining. At this point, you should move on to other areas where you find heavier flow, first tactilely with your hands, then, after considerable experience, by the flowing sense of color.

Now the nonphysical body layers are explored. Reiki is given to any site that has a "lump" in it. Next, I scan the body for physical locations where heavy flow will occur and give Reiki to each of these sites as they are discovered, moving on to the next site when the flow decreases. If time permits the client is asked to lie on his stomach, and the same body scanning technique is used here. Lastly, the client is returned to lying on his back, and a final scan is performed to find any remaining points of high Reiki flow.

At this point, the treatment is completed, and the session is winding down. As a last step, many Reiki 1 healers are taught to "smooth the auras" which they can neither see nor feel. I can't see or feel them either, so I'm skeptical that they even exist. As a result, this step is usually skipped.

The client is now told that the session has ended and that when ready, to sit up. This may take a little help from you, the practitioner, as some clients find it difficult to sit up on the table without a steadying hand to guide the process. The client is then given a bottle of water infused with Reiki to drink on the way home.

Briefly then, here are the steps I use for a typical local Reiki session:

Step 1. Position the client comfortably (lying on his back) on the massage therapy table and note the time from your office clock.

Step 2. Ask the client to close his eyes and give Reiki to the crown and solar plexus chakras to quickly quiet the client.

Step 3. Locate first emotional, then physical stress areas using a full body scan and give Reiki in these places until the flow diminishes.

Step 4. Find sites where stress exists using a full nonphysical body scan, and give Reiki until there is little flow, moving location to location as the flow diminishes at the current location.

Step 5. (If time permits) Scan the client's back for physical stress locations, and give Reiki as needed.

Step 6. End the session. Help the client sit up and offer a bottle of Reiki-infused water.

ABSENT HEALING

Reiki 2 absent healing takes advantage of Reiki's natural nonphysical nature. It can leave the sender and go through the veil into the nonphysical realm. There it identifies when and with whom it is to emerge by matching the symbol of the person to whom (or what) it is being sent as being driven by our intent. Intent in this case includes a date and time for the Reiki energy to appear back into the physical. If no date and time are included, your Reiki will be transmitted and take effect "now."

For those just beginning, Reiki 2 and its absent healing can be, and often are, completely mental. This requires a quiet mind with focused intent for best results and is particularly useful when you are giving absent Reiki when there is someone requesting the absent healing session (and a possible guest). You can send calming Reiki to the visitors as you are working your distant client at the beginning of the session to help minimize their distraction to you.

Effective Reiki 2 cannot be simply "thought of" and that's it, as some Reiki classes imply. The same "physical" protocol is used for absent applications of Reiki 2 energy.

Now, as you're in your Reiki 2 career, try to include some daily meditative practice when possible, however brief. The deeper into a meditation posture you can reach during a healing session, the more effective you will become as a healer.

There are many meditative practices to choose from. If you have no formal meditative experience, I recommend Vipassana meditation as something to try. The reason for this is that this meditational school teaches focused meditation on the sensations felt on and in your body. You will find this very compatible with your Reiki practice where you are focused on the sensations felt by your hands as well as the flow. Ten-day Vipassana retreats are offered in several states. (When applying for retreat attendance, don't mention your Reiki interest—in general these people are very anti-Reiki.)

REIKI 2 PROTOCOL

Reiki 2 operates under the same two spiritual laws that we've already discussed. Also, as before, you still need permission to give Reiki. Obtaining permission to give Reiki using Reiki 2 techniques is slightly more difficult than with Reiki 1 where you can simply ask your client for permission to perform a healing. There are several approaches you can use, and two of them will be mentioned here.

Each treatment begins with you sending the Hon-Sha-Ze-Sho-Nen absent symbol followed by the Cho-Ku-Rei power symbol to your client. Closing your eyes will help you keep focus on your target; a clear visual image or a good symbol or photo of your client is not necessary in this case, but it is nice to have to help visualize the client. Once this takes place, you have a direct link to your client and can now give Reiki to it as if the client was with you in your office.

Again with your eyes closed, draw the absent symbol in the air then the power symbol, watching them form in front of you. When it is complete, watch as it travels to your client, appears over him then slowly sinks in. Next, send the mental or emotional symbol, Sei-Hei-Ki, followed by the Chu-Ku-Rei power symbol. This symbol should be visualized as before, i.e., it travels to the target and slowly sinks into it

Absent healing is driven entirely by intent, and if the absent and power symbols don't reach the client or seem to "bounce off," you should take this as a sign that no permission to heal is granted and immediately end the session. If your symbols disappear into, or are absorbed by, the client, something you can visualize with your eyes closed and your mind quiet, then the link has been established, and you have permission to continue your treatment.

Your treatment can be a "full-body" flash of energy that is over in a few seconds (some argue this is the only way to use Reiki 2), knowing that "Reiki has been sent." Conversely, you can send focused energy to any part of the body by moving your focus from place to place just as you do with your hands in Reiki 1. This type of treatment can last as long as you, the healer, allow it to last. In either case, end the session by sending the Cho-Ku-Rei power symbol over the heart chakra with the intent to end the session and the treatment is finished.

Because of the nonphysical nature of Reiki, it is entirely possible, for example, to send yourself Reiki to take effect tomorrow at 1 p.m. in the conference room. Just follow the protocol as described later and you will discover a different way to perform self-Reiki.

Your intent for a Reiki 2 session doesn't need to be spoken or written although this may help you clarify your target. A photograph or symbol of the person or place receiving the Reiki can be used, placed before you as an aid for focus during the session, but a physical symbol of the target strictly speaking is not necessary. Focus on the target in your "mind's eye" is all that you need.

Using a Teddy Bear

For those just starting out their Reiki 2 experience, when Reiki 2 is being sent for a specific healing, a small teddy bear can be used as a symbol of the client. The bear is good because once the connection is made to your target through the bear, you can scan it as an analog of your client just as if the client is before you, then give your Reiki to those areas on the bear—and thus your client—that are most accepting of your energy. This is difficult to do when using a photograph or other symbol.

Quiet your mind as you begin to tighten your focus on your client-target. Targets can include your bear, client's name, a photo, a drawing or another object serving as a symbol for the client. Ideally, you want to visualize your target with no other thought in your mind. This is the hardest part of the procedure, but with some meditative practice it soon becomes possible, and your Reiki will be more potent as a result.

To establish your connection to the client when using the bear, narrow your focus to the bear's heart chakra, knowing that it symbolizes the heart chakra of your client. Send the absent and power symbols to the bear as described before and thereby your client. The link is now established. Next, send the mental or emotional symbol followed by the power symbol, each time observing the symbol arriving at, then flowing into your client.

You can now do a full-body scan on the bear and pick up on the places where heavy flow can take place on your client. Treat these areas on the bear as if you were giving Reiki to a client on your table by giving Reiki to the heavy draw areas until the flow diminishes at each location.

End the session by first developing the intent to end it, then send a power symbol to the heart chakra of the bear/client and the session is ended.

The Reiki 2 distant or absent practice "works" because metaphysically the symbol of your client, the bear in this instance, becomes one with the client. (See Symbol in Chapter 3) For this reason, during the treatment time, the bear is your client, and so you are actually giving Reiki to your client even though to outside observers it looks like you are merely playing with a teddy bear.

You need no music, incense, or candles to make Reiki 2 work. All that is needed is a quiet space and perhaps a comfortable chair to sit in where you won't be disturbed for the time you are sending Reiki. A quiet, non-ticking clock should be easily seen from this position so you can control the length of the session without moving.

It is also possible to use a human volunteer, or a stick figure, for the target client instead of the teddy bear. With your volunteer on your massage table, quiet your mind and develop your intent to give Reiki to your remote client. As with the teddy bear, send your absent symbol, then the power symbol, tracing them in the air above your volunteer's heart chakra, or, better, do so mentally.

Do your body scan and assessment, then complete your normal Reiki session. Close out the session with that intent to close it followed by the power symbol drawn over the volunteer's heart chakra. It is a happy coincidence that, in this case, both the client and the volunteer will receive your Reiki at the same time, although the heavy flow areas are typically on your client's body, not your volunteer's.

As your experience expands, you will eventually be able to dispense with everything physical, including your teddy bear. All you really need is focus and intent. Thus the whole process becomes mental.

To do this, start comfortably seated in a softly lit room with the door shut, and your telephone/cell phone turned off. Focus your intent on a mental image that represents your client or other target. Allow your focus to narrow without thought until all you can visualize is the client.

Mentally send the absent healing symbol Hon-Sha-Ze-Sho-Nen followed by the power symbol, the Cho-Ku-Rei. Watch in fascination as these symbols fly to your target and are absorbed. Your connection is now established. If you are sending Reiki for an emotional or mental situation, you can now send the Sei-He-Ki mental symbol again followed by the power symbol. (Many Reiki 2 practitioners send the mental symbol as a matter of practice.)

Allow Reiki to flow into your target and run the session for as long as you wish. When you want to end the session establish your closing intent followed by the power symbol above your client's heart chakra.

Another approach is, at the beginning, cup both your hands facing each other. With your focus between them, start your Reiki flowing, sensing it between your hands. In your mind's eye, now place an image of your client between your hands. Gradually open your hands, permitting the image of the client to enlarge until it is, perhaps eighteen to twenty-four inches wide.

Use this image as you did the teddy bear. First, establish the absent connection and scan the image, then send Reiki to those areas accepting of heavy flow. End the session with a power symbol over the heart chakra with the intent to close the session and the session is ended.

HEALING OURSELVES

It is within the illusionary environment of human awareness that we struggle to heal in order to understand the true nature of ourselves. Healing is the function that we experiencing the earth experience are here to live through, healing being the release of restrictions through increased perspective. These restrictions can only be released by experiencing and working through life's learning lessons as established by our incarnational plan. Rather than a curse, these restrictions are available to help us stay on the right course.

Few are aware of these guiding restrictions and many place physical restrictions on themselves in addition to the metaphysically inspired ones. Life constantly presents choices in the form of new opportunities. We have the choice of choosing a new path of adventure whenever one shows up or rejecting it and staying in a more or less comfortable rut.

This doesn't mean that we can live out our days happily in a rut. Incarnationally inspired events will gradually narrow choices until there is no option; the choice to change will either be so compelling that it can't be avoided, or such things as the loss of a cherished job will force a new life direction.

From time to time, clients will show up who are entangled with such choices in front of them and are unsure of which path, if any, they should choose. It is important that the healer avoid giving advice because that advice will always be based on the healer's perspectives rather than the client's. At the beginning of the healing session, the advanced healer will always ask questions that will lead to a specific request for healing. Often times this procedure ends up by the client asking for insight to better understand a problem and help to enlighten the client is what is asked for. The Reiki given during the session then serves to fulfill that realization.

ABSENT HEALING TO YOURSELF

When starting an absent healing, once you are in the quiet, focused state, it is a good time to send yourself some Reiki and enjoy its quiet strength and joy after you have sent Reiki to your client. Visualize the image of the absent healing symbol gently falling into you, followed by the power symbol. Continue to enjoy the focused quiet in your mind as Reiki wraps around you in a gentle, peaceful manner. Bask in its warmth and comfort, then when you are ready, close the session with the Reiki flow slowing to an end as your ending power symbol arrives and is absorbed by your heart chakra.

In Chapter 4, we described how you can make a Reiki Ball, then put your head into it, then stretch it to enclose your entire body. This is a particularly nice, relaxing way to go to bed, safely surrounded by Reiki energy. For Reiki 2 practitioners, the ball will be more resilient if, when it is made, the power symbol is applied, either while it is still in ball form, or after you've entered it.

Another Reiki 2 method for self-Reiki is to use your absent symbol and power symbol with yourself as the target and with the intent that it will send you Reiki at the time and place you desire, such as at bedtime.

If you have a collection of quartz crystals you can also set up a Reiki Machine as described later with yourself as the target symbol. Any of these approaches is perfectly valid, and none is more correct or powerful than another.

Also, there's no reason not to use two or more of these approaches at the same time. Whichever method (or methods) you choose, if you have the Reiki arrive after going to bed, the next morning you'll wake up a bit perkier than usual.

REIKI 2 MACHINES

In Chapter 4, the use of crystals was introduced, detailing uses that all Reiki practitioners can perform with them. Now we return to the subject, this time for those specifically with Reiki 2 training, where absent healings can be augmented through the use of crystals. If you already have your Reiki 2 training and attunements, now would be a good idea for you to review crystal use described in Chapter 4. If you have not yet received the Reiki 2 attunements, the following will be interesting, but won't work for you.

I do not like the term "crystal grid" because it implies that it might represent something new. In short, it doesn't, and so what is described below is a "Reiki Machine." This is far more descriptive of what it is. The concept and entire purpose behind "crystal grids" are functionally the same as the mystical "magic circle." We'll use a circle as being more convenient to draw rather than a "grid" symbol.

The purpose of a "magic" circle is to isolate, and thus protect, the practitioner from the consciousnesses, effects, energies, and fields of the work being done inside the circle. This protection is largely not necessary today as we have reached a level of physicality that precludes much of the work performed by the ancient wizards and sorcerers from having a significant effect on us. But it still has application in energy healing work.

Our use today centers around energy containment. We want all of the stored crystal energy from our crystals to be tightly focused onto the target symbol without losses or energy dissipation through "leaks" in our system. Thus the circle must be drawn as a complete circle without any breaks in it, preferably in one stroke.

The physical marking of the circle is the manifestation of your intent. Its strength lies not in how you draw the circle, but how strong your focus and thereby your intent actually is. You should spend some time quieting your mind and narrowing your focus before drawing the circle. A circle drawn haphazardly with a cavalier attitude will not function nearly as well as one done with focused care and intent. Circles can be reused or run off a copy machine.

SETTING UP A REIKI MACHINE

When we use crystals in conjunction with absent healing Reiki, we draw a circle around the target symbol (a photo or drawing—even a stick figure—is fine) and place three or more cleared "target" crystals spaced around the target. The drawing of the circle can be as simple as a pencil line or as complex as a mosaic pattern on a tile floor. Our intent is that this circle will isolate and contain the crystal energy and that the Reiki absent symbol on the target symbol in the center of the circle is the only doorway for its escape.

If your circle is large enough, you can use your teddy bear as the target symbol, if you're still using the bear. Fundamentally, the bear is not necessary; it is cumbersome when working with a circle which would have to be impractically large. Once you've gotten to the point of using crystals, it is probably time to stop using your teddy and put it back on the shelf anyway.

The client symbol is placed in the center of the circle, along with three or more cleared crystals. Alignment and direction of crystals are not critical, but the crystals should be placed with their sides facing the target symbol. Most of the stored energy in a crystal that you can sense radiates from the sides of the crystal, not, as many assume, from the ends.

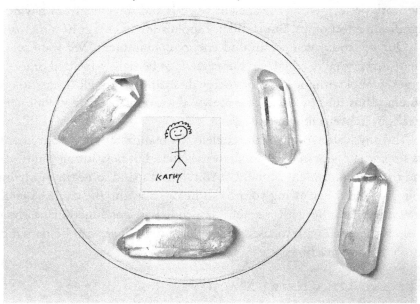

Photo 5-1 After drawing your circle place the symbol of your client or target in the center, in this case, a stick figure representing a person named "Kathy." It was drawn on a Post-it Note so the circle drawing can be used again. The target symbol itself can be a photo or more detailed drawing if you like; there is no advantage of one over the other. The important thing here is to maintain focus and intent. Place your target crystals inside the circle as shown.

The system is started by giving Reiki to the target symbol then establishing an absent Reiki link through it to your client (or other target) using your second-degree Reiki absent healing symbol. Once you have the connection established, apply another power symbol to the target symbol. After this is accomplished, we have a bi-directional link between the target symbol and the object of the target symbol, that is, for whomever or whatever you want to receive your Reiki.

Reiki is now given to the target symbol for a couple of minutes, and then to the target crystals. Probably the best way of "charging up the crystals" is to give your cleared master crystal Reiki with the focused intent that its Reiki is for the target symbol, then transfer that energy to each of the circle's target crystals using the technique described in Chapter 4, Charging Target Crystals.

Once your system is up and running, you should check its operation by passing your freshened sensing hand over the circle. If all is well, the energy emanating from the center of the machine can clearly be sensed above the target symbol inside the circle. If this is not the case, recharge the target crystals and test again. Once running, it is only necessary to recharge the target crystals (in other words, give them Reiki through your master crystal) inside the target circle once or twice a day to keep the machine operating for as long as you wish.

You can sense the machine's overall potency by how "dense" the Reiki is as sensed over the circle. Energy density can also be sensed with your freshened sensing hand by holding it vertically and sweeping it side to side over the center of the machine. This way you can get an idea of the potency by the feeling of "thickness" as your hand passes through the energy field. You may discover that the back of your sensing hand is as sensitive or perhaps more so than the palm side.

You can also judge your machine's activity level by placing your freshened hand horizontally over the center of the circle. Start this scan 2 or 3 feet above the circle, then lowering your hand until activity is sensed. A machine freshly started will typically be sensed about 12 to 24 inches above the center.

RECHARGING THE TARGET CRYSTALS

Recharging target crystals is done by first clearing the master crystal then giving it Reiki to charge it up. Next, the master crystal is touched to each of the discharged target crystals within the circle with the intent to recharge them but also leave the charge in the master crystal. Otherwise, you'll have to recharge the master crystal after each target crystal is charged. Finally, you should check the energy level over the machine to ensure that it has increased appropriately. If your focus is a little out, you may have to give the machine a second charging.

There is no advantage to "over-charging" the target crystals, and there are capacity limits in both the master and target crystals. No ill will comes from over-charging; your Reiki flow into the crystal gradually decreases until there is no flow which happens when the crystal is fully charged.

When using Reiki 2's absent healing ability, the connection to the client (or other target) and the target symbol is nonphysical in nature, and the energy stored in the target crystals flows directly through the symbol and thus to the client in a reasonably efficient manner without significant loss. The subject of increasing the connection flow through increased channel fidelity and client absorption is a subject that we will not cover in this text.

When such a crystal machine is in operation its Reiki energy flow continues twenty-four hours a day until the target crystals' energy is exhausted. If you give the crystal system a booster charge of Reiki once or twice a day using your master crystal, the crystals never completely discharge, and so Reiki can be sent 24/7 with only a little attention on your part.

There is no need to re-establish the link when recharging as long as the target crystals still have energy. Energy will flow to the target as long as the target crystals have some energy left. If your crystals have discharged, you can simply recharge them with your intent, then re-establish your link. After this, your machine will be up and running again.

SHUTTING OFF A REIKI MACHINE

You can shut down a Reiki Machine by simply sending the power symbol to the target symbol with the intent to stop the machine, then remove the target crystals and the target symbol. The crystals should be cleared by washing them in running water then put away. The target symbol and any others you may have placed in the circle should next be removed and disposed of, no need to burn them. Finally, you can put away your circle. You can reuse your circle drawing in later machines if you like; there's no need to make a fresh circle with every machine.

TARGETING WITH A SPECIFIC ENERGY

Often times you'll want to send a specific intent to your target rather than just plain Reiki. For example, you might want to send insight to help the receiver solve a particular problem. Assuming you've established the link, this is easily accomplished by selecting or drawing a symbol for the energy you'd like to send, giving it one or two minutes of Reiki carrying your intent for the symbol, then placing the symbol inside the circle. You are not limited in the number of symbols that you can place inside the circle. Just make sure you've given each symbol Reiki that clearly and definitely establishes its intent before installing it inside the circle.

REMOVING ENERGY FROM YOUR TARGET

This is an empathic subject that most Reiki classes avoid. There are times and situations when you will need to remove energy from a client's body. We are already familiar with draining chakras which begins by opening the lower chakras so energy can flow out, then opening the top chakra and encouraging fresh replacement energy to flow in. We follow a similar procedure when we pull energy out of a client's body.

There are a lot of reasons you may find that you need this particular skill. It can range from pulling bad energy from an infected toenail to draining energy in general from a person who is hyper and going nuts by having so much energy that sleep is impossible.

The Reiki machine makes these procedures much simpler than trying to accomplish it directly or by standard distant healing approaches.

First, you need something to "receive" the bad energy. Any reasonably large stone will work fine as long as you can place it inside the circle.

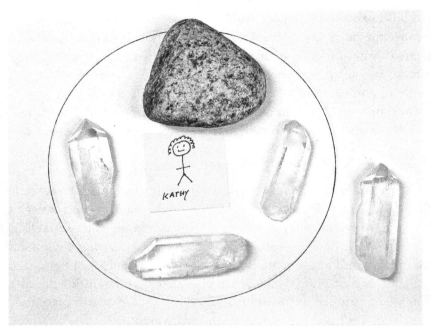

Photo 5-2 Here is a typical setup for distant draining. It is similar to the basic system shown in Photo 5-1 except now a stone is introduced inside the circle. It will receive and hold the energy drained from your client.

Before using the stone it should be discharged and cleansed by washing it under running water in the kitchen sink, the same operation as cleansing your crystals. Dry it then place it in the circle with the intent that it will absorb the bad energy coming from the target.

Next, you need to create a symbol to describe the person (or thing) that you wish to treat. The symbol should have a feature on it that symbolizes the problem you've been asked to treat. For example, if you're treating a bad case of acne, your symbol for the face should have some dots on it, in color if you wish, to symbolize the acne. While drawing and establishing your symbol always remember that, in general, you are trying to treat the root cause of the problem, not the problem itself. The problem is just a symbol of that cause. Recapping from Chapter 3, if you remove the cause, there can be no effect thus healing takes place.

It is your intent that goes through the target symbol to the target (your client), thus transporting your healing effort on the underlying cause of the problem. Also through your intent, "bad" energy will transfer from your client to your stone and be replaced by fresh Reiki energy. Once an underlying problem (a "cause") is successfully resolved the issue that brought the client to your attention will be healed (the "effect").

When the transfer is finished, close down your machine's operation using the procedure described earlier. After this is done, clear your stone by washing it under running water with the intent that it should be cleared, dry it, and put it away after checking to see that there are no energy remnants left in the stone.

TARGETING YOUR ABSENT CLIENT

In all cases, you must focus your absent Reiki healing energy through intent as tightly as possible. For example, let's say that your absent client has a broken arm and you wish to send Reiki directly to the arm as well as any other related locations on the body that are inflamed or torn. You should set up your Reiki machine with a stone to receive the bad energy your intent will encounter.

Your intent must be that your Reiki be sent with this in mind while establishing the connection and that the "bad" energy it encounters will be sent back to the stone. That is all it takes. Intent, as always, is everything.

You may find it advantageous to drain the bad energy directly from the high energy site itself, rather than performing a general draining. If you don't have a stone to receive the bad energy (as shown in photo 5-2), you can drain directly from the absent body. The process is to open the chakras on the feet, then through intent, flush the bad energy out of the body. You can send fresh energy to either the head (the crown chakra) of the client or directly into the high energy site.

Send the healing energy to this site for about five minutes then close the foot chakras, and send a power symbol to the high energy site to terminate further flow. Allow the connection to stay in place. You can at this point continue the session in your normal way. (Leave the crown chakra alone—it will close of its own accord.)

Once your session is completed, your Reiki machine will continue to function. Perhaps on the next day, send a closing power symbol to the client symbol inside the circle with the intent to terminate the flow from the machine. Remove the stone from the circle and clear it by washing it under running water once more. The bad energy will flow away with the water and eventually be returned to the earth. Again, check the stone for any remaining energy before putting it away. Then close down the machine.

Giving a full body Reiki treatment for a well-defined problem is never as effective as finding a location on the body where the Reiki flow is high, then spending time there until the flow falls off. You should then see if you can find another high energy location to focus your energy on. It should be understood that such high energy locations may be some distance on the body from the injury site or affliction that you are dealing with.

TARGET PRACTICE

You can practice targeting your energy by placing three glasses each filled with tap water across the room from you. (Or for convenience you can use bottled water instead.) Number the targets one through three. The object of this activity is to charge one of the targets with Reiki energy while leaving the other two untouched. Randomly select one of the targets to receive your Reiki and write the target's number on a piece of paper. The purpose for this is to clarify your intent and intensify your focus.

At this point, you have several options. You can trace the absent Reiki symbol on the written number (a symbol) of the selected target, followed by the power symbol and your intent that Reiki will flow from your hands to the specified target. Then send it Reiki for a minute or two.

Or you can take your scrap of paper that you just used, place your master crystal on top of it, then use your absent and power symbols over the crystal, and give Reiki to it for a minute or two. This way, your Reiki goes through the crystal where it is transformed to better match the frequency and energy in the appropriate glass or bottle of water. Perform this "water charging" exercise several times.

After each "run," check which of the targets received Reiki and which didn't using your sensing hand. Remember that you're "aiming" for a specific target. Ideally, you'll keep practicing until you can store Reiki energy to the selected target directly from your hands keeping the target symbol "in your head." It will probably take some time and practice to consistently perform this practice, but the exercise is well worth the effort as it can be used on real clients.

Be sure to dump the water from the targets and refill with fresh water or replace any of the bottled water targets that "just happened to" receive your Reiki before your next trial. (For convenience, simply swap out with new bottles of water). Your bottled water can be reused after a day or two have passed and the Reiki energy has dissipated.

WHAT IF IT DOESN'T WORK

We have already described how various minerals have natural "frequencies." Water also happens to have a frequency peculiar to it. If your natural frequency doesn't match up well with water, you'll be in company with many who also find it next to impossible to transfer energy directly to a watery target. This is not due to something you did or didn't do. It is just nature responding the way nature does.

Some healers have a particularly "physical" frequency and work best on clients with a problem of a physical nature. Other practitioners deal best with those with emotional issues. Some can visualize the "colors" of Reiki with eyes closed as it flows through the client. (Most can't see this without serious practice, but some can right away.)

If you aren't able to transfer Reiki energy directly from your hands to a glass of water, don't despair. You can charge up your master crystal by giving it a minute or two of Reiki with the intent to transfer this charge to the glass of water, then touch it to the side of the glass or bottle of water. In this case, the crystal acts as a frequency translator and the target easily absorbs the charge. Be sure to review Chapter 3, Transferring Charge from Crystal to Water.

THE MINERAL MACHINE

Once you are confident in setting up a Reiki Machine, you can modify its performance by using minerals placed in the circle either by themselves or in combination with your target crystals to create a "mineral machine." The concept is that the natural frequency of your minerals is a (sadly, poor) substitute for your master and target crystals, but one that doesn't need charging. The machine will run by itself for as long as it exists.

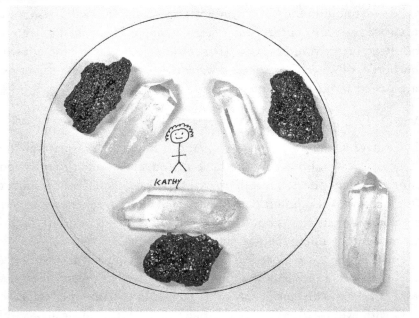

Photo 5-3 A mineral machine setup. Mineral samples are placed outside the target crystals as shown. Once your link to the target is established, energy from the minerals is transmuted by the target crystals to be better absorbed by your target. This machine will run unattended until dismantled after which the target crystals should be cleansed under running water to clear them of residual energy.

Start the machine by placing the target symbol in the center of the circle. Cupping it between your hands, send it the absent symbol followed by the power symbol to establish the link. Now place your *discharged* target crystals around the target symbol with the sides facing the target symbol. Then charge them one by one using your master crystal which you have charged with the intent that the targets are to translate the mineral energy into one that your target can best use.

Finally, place your minerals inside the circle but *outside* the target crystals. Finish by giving the machine one more power symbol with the intent that it function to the betterment of your target. At this point, your mineral machine is up and running, and you can check its operation by sensing the energy above the target symbol.

If you feel that the machine isn't putting out a significant amount of energy, give it another round of Reiki. This is often the case because mineral machines are naturally weaker than true Reiki machines. When you are finished with the machine, an orderly shutdown should be used. End the absent connection by placing the intent of closing down the machine and the power symbol on the target. Next remove the minerals that are in place, then finally the target crystals. If you are curious about what happens during the shutdown, you can check the energy above the machine as you disassemble it.

The mineral machine does not have the high output of a standard Reiki machine, as you can tell by sensing the energy over the top of the circle. But it also doesn't need to be tended to as does a Reiki machine. If you have an interest in such "self-activated" machines, you can try different mineral specimens or even mix them. The possibilities for different combinations are nearly endless.

The stand-alone mineral machine has two major flaws. First, the problem of having to match the "frequency" of the ailment being treated and that of the mineral being used as the energy source without your healing intent. Second, a diagnosis must be made before a proper cure can be dispensed. We overcame these objections by using your target crystals to translate the natural mineral frequency to match your intent given to the target crystals. An advantage of the mineral machine is that it requires little attention once it is running. But generally, you'll find better flow by using a standard Reiki Machine.

A Duplex Reiki Machine

You can set up a "duplex" Reiki machine by adding another set of crystals to a standard setup. In the case of Photo 5-4, three rose quartz crystals are shown set outside the target crystals. This will broaden frequency translation capability of the machine, making it more sensitive to the Reiki "frequency" that is loaded when starting up the machine.

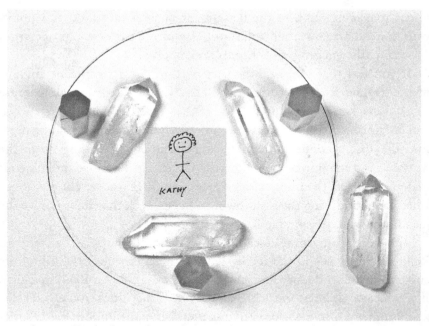

Photo 5-4 A duplex Reiki machine. In this case, two types of quartz crystal are used to increase its "frequency range" that some healers find helpful due to their internal frequency being outside that accepted by their crystal set.

The extra set of crystals used in a duplex machine does not significantly increase its output power. The effect is at the input to the machine where they accept and translate incoming energy on a different frequency range than plain quartz crystals. In this manner, they increase the bandwidth of the machine to include incoming energy that would ordinarily not be useable.

Problems with the Mind

The biggest problem that you'll encounter with Reiki and mineral machines is that your mind will logically try to stop you from even trying to make one. It can't cope with the unseen and unheard. In many cases, it will try to stop you from even drawing the circle for the machine.

It will ridicule and degrade you by telling you that you're stupid for even thinking these machines might work. You can temporarily disable your mind from this by simply refusing to think. After it sees that the machine does work (because you sensed the energy above the target symbol) it will quiet down, but only for a little while. The next time you check your machine, your mind will again raise its ugly head and have to be stifled once more.

Because of this mind noise, many Reiki healers never bother to experiment with crystals. This is understandable as there is a lot of New Age hype of questionable value that gives your mind plenty of ammunition to bombard you with. And since traditional Reiki classes don't show how to use crystals or even how to sense energy or energy flow with your hands, your mind will further belittle you for trying out these techniques or even thinking about trying them.

However, the methodology described here demonstrates that they do work, and so at the very least, it is something worth looking into. Suitable crystals for use in Reiki machines are relatively inexpensive. You don't need large "museum quality" crystals. Perfectly good "by the pound" crystals selected for about 2-1/2" in length at the time of purchase work well as shown in the photos above.

As described, mineral and Reiki machines can be a powerful adjunct to any Reiki practice, particularly in that of the advanced Reiki healer. They can be used as unattended stand-alone systems or can be used alongside a practitioner who is also giving absent Reiki to the same target.

There is almost no limit to their versatility and usefulness in the healing art.

REIKI IN TIME AND SPACE

Reiki, as conventionally taught, is used for healing clients, which includes humans as well as other life forms, such as family pets. But in addition to animals and plants, Reiki 2 can be used for environmental purposes, to quiet or calm tense situations or to bring peace in combative situations.

It is particularly useful for situations both present and in the future. It has very limited use for things in the past. Generally speaking, it is not possible to alter events in the past to the advantage of us in the present or future. For example, Reiki cannot save someone dying from the Plague in the past because to do so would impress changes into the present. This has all the makings of science fiction and time travel. But for things of a happenstance nature taking place in the present or that will in the future, Reiki can be of considerable use.

Although Reiki can be used to affect events in the future, it cannot be used to gain an unfair advantage over others, for that would be a violation of Spiritual Law. (See Healing and Spiritual Law in Chapter 4) But it can be used to help both yourself as a healer and clients to be calm and to do our best work in difficult or tense moments.

For example, suppose that you were asked to do a presentation next week about Reiki, and being in front of a crowd always makes you tense and somewhat uncomfortable. Reiki can help with your anxiety in two ways. First, it can send calming energy to you during your presentation and second, it can help center your audience's attention on your presentation so that the crowd itself is not as much of a distraction to you.

Two approaches can be used in cases like this. First, you can send absent Reiki to yourself and the audience in the future with the intent that it last throughout your presentation. Or, you can set up a Reiki machine to send Reiki to yourself, your audience and the room or hall in which your presentation is to take place. Or you can do both.

In setting up for the event, you will have much better results if you take the time to set up a "session" for yourself the same as if you were working for a client. Become comfortable in a chair then carefully focus on the results you wish as you step through the procedure given above for an absent healing. In this case, you are after a calming effect and an attentive, appreciative audience rather than an ordinary "healing." Because you're dealing with mental aspects of both you and your client, you should use the mental symbol with the intent to blanket the audience, the room or hall, and yourself.

Once you have established your link, send the mental/emotional symbol followed by the power symbol since you are requesting calmness which is an emotional state. Next, phrase your desired outcome in as simple terms as you can, being specific as to time, date and location, followed by the power symbol. Continue by expressing your request two or more times, ending each "statement" with the power symbol. You must take care to state your request exactly the same for each "pass," otherwise your intent will be defused and not be as effective as it can be.

When it is time to end the session place a power symbol on your target, then close your hands with the intent that the session is finished.

INITIALIZING A REIKI MACHINE

Setting up a Reiki machine to do the same job as above has certain benefits but requires some care. Once set up and loaded with your request, it will establish a link that forms during the time and date that you've requested. You can change or modify your request at any time prior to the date and time it is to take effect.

Set up a basic Reiki machine in the same manner as previously described. In this case, you need to find something to use as the symbol for the place the Reiki is intended to arrive. This can be a simply drawn building with an arrow symbolically marking the appropriate room. If there is a room number, include that on your symbol. Again, specifics are very important as your request will be quite literally interpreted. (See below.)

Next, you need a symbol for your audience. Again, a simply drawn symbol will work. This will serve as part of your target symbol. And finally, you need a symbol that indicates the time period the machine is to be active. You can hand draw the symbols or cut pictures out of a newspaper. Remember, it is your intent that these images symbolically represent your target that is important. With these symbols now placed around the target symbol in the center of your circle, cleanse and drain your target crystals then place them inside the circle around the symbols.

You can activate the machine any time before it is time to start operation. Cleanse your master crystal and, cupping it in your hands, give it Reiki for a few moments followed by the power symbol. Over your symbols in the center of the circle, send the absent Reiki symbol followed by the power symbol, thus establishing the link. Carefully phrase your request followed by the power symbol, then do the same with the emotional/mental symbol. Charge each of the cleansed target crystals from your master crystal then set your master crystal aside. Your Reiki machine is now operational.

You should spend considerable time practicing the setting up of a machine that gives Reiki to a bottle of water at a given time and place. Such practice will give you the confidence to overcome the objections of your mind, objections that can stop your practice entirely if allowed to remain festering in your thoughts.

REIKI REQUESTS

As you deal with the metaphysic, which includes Reiki, you must be very careful in phrasing your requests because of the literal interpretation that takes place in the nonphysical. It is not possible for the nonphysical to decode implied or inferred meanings, and this has historically been a problem for those who work in this field.

When sending absent Reiki to yourself to arrive sometime in the future, it is vitally important that your request be carefully and precisely formed as to date, time and location. If there is any ambiguity in your request such as the date or time your Reiki may not arrive at the time and place that you intended.

Requests should use simply stated sentences without mixed meanings. Also, when requesting Reiki for oneself, it is not a bad idea to write out your request before your session begins. This will help clarify your request and expose language that the nonphysical cannot properly handle.

It is possible to have a linguistically correct request and still have problems with the nonphysical interpretation of it. Take for example the following request:

I need more energy at a quarter of 10 tomorrow.

Properly phrased it comes out more like this:

Send me more energy starting at 9:45 a.m. and ending at 10:30 a.m. tomorrow morning.

This statement now explicitly and unambiguously states what is wanted and precisely when it should be fulfilled. The time of the request is now specifically set to start tomorrow morning at 9:45 and end at 10:30. The original request was ambiguous when it describes a need, not an action item. And the term "quarter of 10" doesn't specify whether the time is in the morning or late evening. Further, the term "quarter" is not clear—a quarter of what? A dollar? And finally, it did not describe a time frame over which the Reiki energy is to take effect.

Notice that we do not "beg" in our requests. Begging only confuses the nonphysical, and would sound something like this:

"Please give me more energy at 9:45 tomorrow morning."

Our requests, either for ourselves or our clients, must always stipulate exactly what is wanted and when it is to occur and over a specific time period. The above statement is unclear as to what the practitioner wants, when it is wanted, and over what period of time it is to manifest.

We've already noted that Reiki itself does not "make somebody do something" because that would be a violation of Spiritual Law. It can, however, help someone to see the benefits of changing an attitude either at the conscious state or at some level of unconsciousness. After that, it is up to the person whether or not to change. It can also help people who are struggling with problems at home or at work. It does this by giving insight, perspective, reinforcement, and support. It cannot of itself solve the problem, but it can help make good decisions.

Reiki energy is entirely of a mental or nonphysical nature. Reiki could be sent to, say, a rusting old bridge with the intention to stop, or better yet, reverse the rusting, but this won't happen. Reiki energy only affects living beings of one nature or another.

Reiki can be given to pets or other animals. It works best if you can quickly scan the animal for locations of heavy Reiki flow before going ahead. In most cases, the animal will show signs of receiving it. Animal responses range from lying down and going sleep to becoming feisty. Or there may be no apparent response at all. It all depends on the animal.

And finally, Reiki can only be effective if the requests are allowed by the incarnational plan of the receiver. Like all other energy entering a being it must first pass through the incarnational filter before its energy can be recognized and utilized.

GIVING REIKI WITHOUT THE SYMBOLS

Memorizing the Reiki symbols and names of symbols can be a challenge. Happily, Reiki is intent-driven, meaning that it operates when you intend for it to be there, even when you haven't had the time to cleanly draw out the symbols. However, repeating the names for the symbols silently in your mind and "drawing" them on your hands helps maintain focus on your intent especially if you're new to the Reiki practice.

After you have had a little experience with the absent Reiki symbols, manually drawing them out will become unnecessary. When your intent is formed, and you have spoken the symbol names several times in your head, the symbol is complete in your intent, and it will rapidly transfer to your intended target and meld into it. Once this happens, it isn't necessary to keep repeating its name because the link has been made.

GIVING REIKI AS A MEDITATION

Giving Reiki by whatever means requires focused intent. It is a given that you need to quiet your mind for this to happen for consistently good results. The best way to do this varies from one healer to the next, but the point is to stop the mind's constant chatter both before and during the healing session as much as possible.

The mind will at first be difficult to deal with. However, if you make time for a little meditation practice every day, it will soon become much easier to control. When the quiet and peace of meditation becomes a part of your daily routine your day will start without stress.

The meditation should start off with you sitting as comfortably as possible. Avoid trying to meditate while lying down as one tends to fall asleep in this posture. Close your eyes, and for a moment, listen to the endless chatter coming from your mind. It is this chatter that we want to end.

There are several types of mind relaxation methods that are easily mastered. One method is to listen to what the mind is saying for a few moments. Notice how it changes thoughts because it knows you're listening in on it. Keeping your focus on the mind, force it to stop thought, and for a few moments feel what it is like to be completely in the moment without thought. Every time a thought begins to appear, stop it without thought. Practice this approach for ten or fifteen minutes, preferably at the start of the day.

Another method is, in your mind's eye and as an example, to create the most perfect apple you have ever seen. Keep your focus on the apple without thought. Let the apple slowly start to rotate in one direction, then the other. Go above the apple and look down at its stem as it is turning. Let the apple rotate end over end so you can eventually see the bottom of it. Try not to think while this is going on. Once you've mastered the apple allow it to fade, leaving your mind completely blank.

You can also focus your intent on your body in order to quiet your mind. From your comfortable position, focus on the end of your nose, witnessing your breath as it draws in, then goes out. Keep your mind focused like this for ten or fifteen minutes. When it starts to wander off, bring it back on task without self-criticism or thought.

There are many other methods for training the mind to be quiet including audio programs such as those mentioned earlier in chapter 2, the Monroe Institute (www.monroeinst.org) and Centerpointe Research Institute (www.centerpointe.com) products.

Sending Yourself Reiki Using the Absent Symbol

Once your mind is quiet by whatever meditational scheme you are using, you're ready to send Reiki to yourself, someone else, or an object using the following steps:

Step 1. Form your request. This can be as simple as, "Help me be more focused on the new project at work all day tomorrow" for example. Or you can request calming Reiki to reach you some time in the future, perhaps at an important meeting: "Help me to be totally relaxed and alert at next Friday's meeting between 10 a.m. and 11 a.m." Notice that these requests are statements of what you want and when and where you want the Reiki to take effect. In this case, we want to be more focused "tomorrow at work," detailing how you will be feeling after the Reiki takes effect rather than, "I wish to be more focused at work." That request doesn't indicate on what you want to be more focused. Requests should always include a "what, when and where" in them.

Step 2. Send the absent symbol (Hon-Sha-Ze-Sho-Nen) followed by the power symbol (Cho-Ku-Rei), while focusing on yourself. Repeat the symbol names several times to help narrow your focus. As you are doing this, in your mind's eye and without thought, draw the symbols so they are standing in front of you, then allow them to come forward and wash into your body, one after another.

Step 3. Wait a minute or so, then do the same with the mental symbol (Sei-He-Kei) followed by another power symbol, repeating the symbol names several times.

Step 4. Continue to send yourself Reiki in this manner until you feel you are finished, perhaps five minutes or so, then send the power symbol one last time, repeating its name several times as you close your hands together with the intent that you are closing down the session.

SENDING ABSENT REIKI TO A PERSON OR OBJECT

This process is similar to sending absent Reiki to yourself except at the beginning we first focus on the target, who should be relaxed in a comfortable, quiet area (wherever the target is), followed by the intent. After sending each symbol, you should silently speak its name several times, as just described, this to aid keeping your intent focused.

Step 1. Cup your hands around the symbol of the target you wish to send Reiki to, then send the absent symbol (Hon-Sha-Ze-Sho-Nen) followed by the power symbol (Cho-Ku-Rei). Observe the symbols as they travel to and are absorbed by the target. This establishes your connection to the target. If the symbols aren't absorbed by the target, you do not have permission to give it Reiki.

Step 2. Send the mental symbol (Sei-Hei-Ki) followed by the power symbol. (This step is optional if your target hasn't requested a healing of a mental nature.)

Step 3. Focus now on the request for a few moments and mentally send it followed by the power symbol. Again, the request should be phrased on how the target will feel or be after the Reiki session has ended.

Step 4. Maintain the Reiki flow as long as you feel it being absorbed by the target or until you want to end the session.

Step 5. Close the session by sending one more power symbol over the heart chakra with the intent that the session is ended.

The procedures given above are simply examples of how absent healing can be given. You are encouraged to try them out, modifying them to suit your particular needs. We've barely touched on the most common uses of absent Reiki. With just a little effort and experience you'll quickly discover what works best for you.

You will probably discover that the background music that you play during a session helps to more quickly get you into a quiet, meditative state. And if you work on your meditative skills using either of the two audio programs already mentioned, your progress will accelerate even more quickly. (In these cases no background music should be played.)

GIVING ABSENT REIKI

When giving absent Reiki, we've so far described having a symbol on which to focus. The symbol need not be something physical because with a little practice it can be visualized in your mind's eye. The process begins by cupping your hands together and visualizing the target as being inside your cupped hands. Your hands will probably warm as the process continues. The following steps detail an absent session:

Step 1. Send the absent symbol to your target mentally, then the power symbol. Your link to the target is now complete. Send the mental symbol followed by the power symbol if appropriate. Gradually open your hands stretching the target and expanding it between them.

Step 2. Position the hands eighteen to twenty-four inches apart. Once your hands are in place, your target can be scanned, and high flow areas can be detected. You can also scan the nonphysical bodies, looking for "lumps" which should receive Reiki as a matter of practice. Keep scanning the body looking for and servicing areas of high energy flow.

Step 3. Continue giving Reiki by focused intent until the session time has run out or you feel that you've done all you can for this session.

Step 4. Close down the session by slowly bringing your hands together at which time you should give the target one last power symbol with the intent that the session is over.

It should by now be apparent that the main difference between local and absent Reiki is the use of the distant and mental symbols to establish the link. Once the link is in place, Reiki can be given in the normal way, even though we're using a symbol for the client's body. The teddy bear described earlier served the same purpose as the metaphysical target held between your hands.

OUT OF BODY EXPERIENCES

Only rarely will a client describe an "out of body" experience where it seems like his consciousness "floated" out of the body up toward the ceiling and was free to look around the room, explore the building he was in or briefly wander about outside.

In the several times this has happened when I was giving Reiki, no particular change in flow occurred, and there was no indication that anything out of the ordinary had happened. It was discovered only after the session had ended and the client volunteered that the event took place.

Reports of such occurrences should be taken seriously, and you should allow the client to describe as much about the experience as he is willing. Such experiences can be verified, if you desire, by gently asking the client to describe things in the room that could not be seen from your therapy table. You should tell the client that a very rare occurrence took place and that you appreciate being told about it.

Also, explain that such occurrences sometimes take place during surgeries when patients are anesthetized. Recent research has analyzed the brain activity in the participants' temporal and parietal lobes, which are involved in spatial perception and the feeling of owning one's body, during surgery. When these areas are more active, some mind-body dis-association can take place. Medical research is studying the phenomenon which may be partially explained by unusual brain activity. In any event, let your client know that it probably won't happen again and that you hope that the experience wasn't frightening.

SPIRITS

Dealing with spirits at the healer level is something that sooner or later every healer will be faced with: what do you do when you encounter a spirit on or in your client?

Infrequently, a client who has an unwelcomed attached spirit comes to the attention of advanced healers. Such spirits can come from two sources. First, they can be spontaneously exposed as the result of rapid growth and change, or second, they can come in as a free unassigned spirit. Spirits can be benign, or they can maliciously attack your client, with all sorts of behaviors in between.

We're not talking about "spooks" that you meet on Halloween; we are talking about the real thing, a spiritual possession. On the face of it, you might want to avoid the problem when it is encountered and leave the spirit attached to your client.

This is an unsatisfactory solution, as your client came to you for a healing and you agreed to do it. Leaving an attached spirit can be damaging to your client, and it is unlikely to leave of its own accord. Under these circumstances, the problems your client is experiencing will only get worse, and in extreme cases can cause a loss of job and family.

Conventional medicine cannot help as it may treat your client with anti-psychotic drugs that affect the brain and are totally ineffective at spirit removal. Spirits are ethereal, that is, they operate from the non-physical side of things, something that Western medicine cannot handle.

So it is up to you, the healer, to rid your client of these pests. You might not feel able to do anything about it, but spiritual law is on your side. Once again, Spiritual Law is:

1. *No spirit has the right to interfere with the free will of another.*
2. *No spirit has the right to impose a debt onto another.*

You know the first law and so does the attached spirit. Thus there can be no argument or discussion about its continued interfering with your client.

Spiritual Possession

In most cases, spiritual possession is not truly malicious, although it is never appropriate or beneficial for one to entertain an attached spirit for any longer than necessary. Attached spirits drain energy to support themselves or cause various kinds of mischief and mental confusion. Muddled thinking, the inability to properly concentrate or remember details, "dual thoughts" (two or more thoughts running at the same time), groundless panic or anger attacks, inappropriate behavior, and speech, often in the form of embarrassing language or innuendo, are the common psychological effects stemming from a spiritual possession.

Typical physical effects include chronic fatigue, irregular heartbeat and breathing difficulties (particularly at night), fitful and restless sleep often coupled with vivid and stressful dreams, clumsiness and a propensity for accidents of all kinds. When a spirit is particularly anxious to leave, there are often sensations all over the body in the form of prickles or of the skin "crawling." These sensations can take place anytime during the day or night.

For healers themselves and those they heal, possession sometimes comes as the natural result of rapid and perhaps unexpected spiritual growth. Occasionally, this releases an embedded or lower layer consciousness serving a designated but completed role in the current incarnation. Other unintentional possessions take place when a spirit is inadvertently trapped in the body. This sometimes results when one or more spirits compete for a particular body at birth, or during an event such as an accident or illness, when the rightful spirit is temporarily absent from the body and an opportunistic spirit tries to take it over.

A similar situation takes place with those who have latent medium talents. When the medium channel is uncontrolled and happens to close while a visiting spirit is resident, it becomes trapped.

Spiritual possession typically takes place when a less than saintly spirit chooses to interfere with a particular incarnation, only to find itself trapped, a result of its action for violating spiritual law. Happily, most attached spirits, including the interfering types, are more than willing to leave and do so voluntarily when "shown the door." This is a gentle, empathic healing process that benefits both the spirit and those temporarily hosting them.

True spiritual emergencies can also be a serious consequence of uninformed client exploration. These can also spontaneously manifest in cases where psychic openings of one type or another suddenly occur, typically to an unsuspecting person with latent psychic or mediumistic abilities.

There is a dark side to spiritual possession. In extreme cases, the attaching spirit becomes malicious leading to any number of abnormal psychological states. Stanislav Grof's 1989 book, *Spiritual Emergency: When Personal Transformation Becomes a Crisis* (ISBN 0-87477-538-8) outlines many of the more common abnormal states that can occur. He describes how patients undergoing a spiritual event may be misdiagnosed as psychotic in one of several ways. Naturally, treatments for such diagnoses are ineffective at removing the spirit or spirits.

The more advanced the spirit is, the greater the potential danger is for your client. Referral to the traditional medical psychiatry system will not be helpful if they are facing a genuine case of possession. Traditional psychotic medications given are typically anti-depressants, anti-psychotics, sedatives, and counseling. These may temporarily give some signs of improvement, but nothing long term will work in possession cases. It should be noted that psychiatry makes no distinction between psychosis and mysticism.

Of the two types of attachment, those resulting from growth and change are generally easy to treat, and it is this form of possession that I will address. Treating foreign or outside possessions can be accomplished in a similar manner, but will not be discussed here. Those who have unaddressed major spiritual problems can contact the Spiritual Emergence Network (described in Grof's book) for referrals and other assistance on the web at www.spiritualemergence.info.

SPIRITS FROM WITHIN

Those clients who are actively pursuing rapid personal growth often advance so quickly that an embedded spirit is spontaneously released inside the body. And it is nearly always the case that there will be some "buddies" (lesser parasite spirits) that accompany the one that is causing the mischief, and these must be addressed as well.

It is better to release all of these spirits at once rather than one by one, spreading it out over time. The reason for this is that the lesser spirits may not be so easily led out of the body. They are good at following a larger spirit but are somewhat lost if isolated from a leader.

Spirit release generally takes about a half hour to complete. It is a benign treatment that will not make things worse if it fails. These spirits are relatively small energy centers and usually respond well to this form of treatment. Rarely do these types of spirits engage in major mischief, but they can affect one's ability to clearly think or feel rested after a (probably) restless night's sleep.

A spiritual release session begins the same as a normal healing session. The healer, however, might suspect a spiritual possession based on the results of the interview held at the beginning of the session. A standard body scan is used, but in this case, the healer also scans for potential spirits through focused intent with the freshened hand. Indications for a spirit vary. They sometimes feel "springy" or "lumpy," and in many, if not most cases, they move around as the scanning proceeds.

A general sense of the size of the spirit that is involved can be ascertained during the scan. Just make sure that well-focused intent is maintained while searching for the spirit. Otherwise, other energy centers and the chakras may be located instead.

The client may be able to explain in general terms where a spirit is presently located. (This should come out in your interview prior to the start of your session.) This is nice information to know, but in general, it is not necessary; you will locate the spirits involved during your scan anyway.

SPIRIT REMOVAL PROTOCOL

This protocol can be used on oneself or on a client, using either absent Reiki or Reiki by touch. It should take place in a quiet room with all distractions (telephone, cell phone, etc.) turned off or disabled. Background music commonly used for healing sessions is optional. If removing the spirits absently, use your Reiki absent healing symbol (Hon-Sha-Ze-Sho-Nen) followed by the power symbol (Cho-Ku-Rei) to link up with your client then follow the above by sending your mental symbol (Sei-He-Ki) and another power symbol. This is necessary to make the spirits more physical, so they can better be manipulated.

Otherwise, use your normal Reiki scanning procedure. In either event, the spirits you are looking for are typically hiding somewhere on the torso, so you'll need to carefully scan the body to find them. Once found, address them, (a simple hello is sufficient) then send healing Reiki to the spirit or spirits that you are working with.

Addressing these spirits, the healer says (out loud—they cannot hear your thoughts) that they are in the wrong place and must leave now. Also, that you are sending Reiki energy to help them move on to the escape channel. You, and especially your client, should start to feel or sense "movement" as the spirits begin to move toward the crown chakra.

Using your freshened scanning hand and sensing intent verify that there is spirit energy around your client's head. Addressing your client, ask that the escape channel be opened. Addressing the spirits, while continuing to supply Reiki, tell them that the escape channel is now open and that they are free to move through it without fear.

Your client will, of course, not have any idea of what an escape channel is, so explain that it should be imagined as a large pipe with a big faucet on it. When asked to open the channel, imagine turning the faucet "on," and to turn it off when the channel is to be closed.

You should be able to sense movement of these spirits either by feeling the movement with your Reiki or by scanning with your freshened hand. If necessary, give the spirits further encouragement to leave, explaining that both they and you know they don't belong in your client's body and that now is the time to leave.

When you feel or sense that the spirits have gone, ask your client to close the escape channel. At this point, you can stop giving Reiki ending with the power symbol and by withdrawing your hands if your client is local.

Your client will typically feel some immediate beneficial effect. You should caution your client against meddling with the escape channel as it could allow in a new spiritual infestation. And if appropriate remind your client that playing with spiritual "things" such Ouija™ boards is not a good idea and can result in another spiritual attachment.

The effects of this procedure vary in the short term. Some clients may not feel anything at all, others have vivid memories of the entire process. The effects of this process will continue to show improvement in your client over the next day or two.

REMOVING SPIRITS FROM ONESELF

Spirit removal from oneself follows the protocol just described. This time, you can use standard Reiki (absent Reiki treatment is not required) to "herd" the spirit or spirits up towards your crown chakra. You must still address the spirits vocally because they can't hear your thoughts despite being inside you, the healer.

Once they are near your crown chakra, open your escape channel and tell them to leave. Close the escape channel once they are gone, or at least once you feel that they are gone. You should do a body scan to make sure all of your attached spirits have left. Sometimes one or two "little ones" are left behind, so you should escort them to the escape channel and let them out as well. Close the escape channel after the last of the spirits have left.

Despite its simplicity, spirit removal is not a trivial exercise. The clients that come to you with this sort of problem may be desperate for relief from the insanity of a full-blown possession, and medical science has not been able to help them. The above protocol is given as an example of any number of ways to remove spirits; there are many other procedures that can be used. It is up to you, the healer, to explore and find the methodology that you are most comfortable with. As always you should consider the above as a starting point for your practice, not the destination.

As a general comment, there are classes of spirits that will not respond to this protocol. Of particular concern are those of the demonic persuasion. In worse cases, they sometimes respond by putting on a truly frightening display. DO NOT ATTEMPT TO REMOVE SUCH DEMONS YOURSELF. The individual should be directed to a priest who can perform an exorcism. This exercise is not for the inexperienced healer to attempt to resolve.

Reviewing, the steps for removing a spirit (or spirits) are:

Step 1. Relax your client, giving Reiki to the spirit(s) to help them move upward to the escape channel. Follow with Reiki below the spirits, keeping them between your Reiki and the client's head. This is a "herding" maneuver, that is, herding the spirit(s) to the escape channel.

Step 2. Ask your client to open the escape channel through which the spirits can exit without damage. (Suggest that the client just imagine opening a valve on a pipe near the top of the head.)

Step 3. Ask your client to close the escape channel once the spirits(s) are gone.

Step 4. Give your client some calming Reiki. The process of spirit removal is not painful but can cause some anxiety.

Step 5. Help your client sit up on the therapy table, and the treatment is finished.

It goes without saying that it would be best to receive first-hand training in this subject area given by a Reiki Master or senior-level psychic who has substantial experience in removing spirits. Such practitioners are typically hard to locate in less than urban environments. And once found it is up to you to discover the Master's background and actual experience. Don't be bashful—ask for references if you have any doubts.

REIKI AND EMPATHIC HEALING

At this point, we've covered how healing energy can be transferred from yourself, the healer, to another who has asked for a healing. This is a largely one-way transference where the healer can only sense whether or not the client is accepting the energy or how the flow is progressing. With considerable experience, we can discern if the healing is progressing by sensing the flow as it reaches the client and is dispersed within the body.

Some healers work as empaths. Here the healer transfers the *illness* energy from the client to himself. This is not a healing role to be taken lightly as the healer's body must first experience the discomfort brought on by the illness and only then begin to heal itself. Natural empaths often lead an uncomfortable life, particularly in their junior years, until they discover a means to "shut off" the illnesses that surround them especially in schools and crowded public areas.

We previously described an illness as a restriction caused by a collision between the life currently being led and one's incarnational imperative. An energy healing brings about the insight and perspectives necessary to one's life so that it can move forward in a more incarnationally appropriate direction.

Once this happens, the illness in the client is no longer necessary, and because the life has been brought back on track, it vanishes. Because the energy transfer is only *from* the healer *to* the client, no harm or physical discomfort to the healer takes place.

Empathic healing and *empathic* techniques are different. Here the *illness energy*, that is the energy being used to sponsor the illness in the client, is deliberately transferred from the client's body to that of the healer's. As the healing in the client progresses, the illness from the client's body moves to that of the healer who then experiences the same pain or suffering as the client was feeling. But because the transferred energy does not "belong" to the healer, it is rejected and eventually consumed by the healer's body.

The energy being transferred to the healer, in this case, is the energy *blocking* the insight and perspectives from being gained by the client. Once this energy is removed, insight and perspective naturally flow into the client who then becomes "healed."

In the meantime, the healer assumes and experiences all the pain and discomfort held by the client until the healer's body processes and discards it. For minor issues, the length of time the empathic healer experiences the illness is short, perhaps as long as up to an hour or two. But for major issues, the effects may be felt for a week or longer. For this reason, using an empathic approach to healing should not be taken lightly. At times, it can be very uncomfortable.

Because empathic healing takes place by the healer opening up to allow the energy flow to enter the body, young empathic healers often suffer from many illnesses, both short and long-term during the early years. These continue until the healer learns to protect himself by "shutting down" when not actively conducting a healing to prevent unwanted energy exchanges from happening.

This is particularly important as the empath is usually very sensitive to the immediate surrounding environment. "Crowd noise" can cause a variety of illnesses that can last from hours to several days. The empath can be shielded by use of a number of Reiki tools. These must be brought to bear prior to exposure. Encircling the empath's body in a Reiki ball as described in Chapter 4 is usually quite effective but not always practical to apply.

Also, the use of Reiki 2's absent healing strategies is effective. Here, Reiki shielding energy can be made to "show up" at a particular time and place. Probably the best Reiki tool for sustained Reiki protection can be set up with a Reiki crystal machine. Instead of being limited to a specific time and place, the crystal machine can track the empath, providing Reiki protection throughout the working day.

Shutting down and opening up for an empathic healing is a matter of controlled intent. It is the same process used in Reiki 2 healings where the flow for a connection is accomplished by intent. For a local or hands-on empathic healing to take place, the healer first gently places his hands over the site most sensitive to the illness (or anywhere on the body when no localized site is apparent), then by intent alone, opens up to allow the energy to start flowing from the client into his body.

When the healer wants to close the session, he removes his hands coupled with the intent that the treatment is finished, thus closing down the flow if it is still active. Energy flow in empathic healings can vary in intensity, the same as with Reiki and other energy healing modalities. The main distinction is the *direction* of flow, that is, from the client to the healer.

For absent empathic healings, the healer brings focus to a symbol (photo or drawing of the target), then by intent alone starts the flow from the client and at the same time opens up to receiving that energy. The treatment can last as long as there is flow or as long as the healer wishes it to last. The session is ended by removing the intent thus closing down the flow.

An alternative empathic approach is to establish contact with the client using the standard Reiki 2 protocol, then instead of sending Reiki energy, by intent start the energy flow from the client to oneself. At this point, the empathic healer allows his body to absorb and disperse the incoming energy. For reference on draining techniques see Draining Exercises in Chapter 2. Also, the empathic energy flow can be directed to a large stone as used in Reiki 2 remote draining technique, (see Photo 5-2) rather than the healer's body.

There is the possibility that the flow doesn't start at all and the healing attempt fails. The same possibility exists for standard Reiki draining exercises. Using a stone rather than the empath's body is infinitely more comfortable for the healer, but the tradeoff is that the empath is "outside the loop" and has no way of knowing how the energy exchange is progressing.

Empathic healing sessions are terminated through the intent of the healer. Once the session is ended, the energy stored in the stone should be washed from it and down the drain, the same as if the stone was used for a draining exercise. This approach should be used with care because the flow going into the stone cannot be monitored.

Thus there are distinctive similarities between Reiki and empathic approaches, these being primarily in the session initiation and termination practice. It is important to maintain the intent of what is to happen during the session in any energy healing attempt. Without focused intent, neither Reiki nor empathic healings can be effective.

The Final Frontier

After steadily working with Reiki for a few years and with considerable meditation during this time, the advanced healer will enter a new phase of experience as the use of symbols becomes unnecessary. And the use of Reiki machines and crystals will be largely dropped as being too much of a bother to set up and work with.

This is possible because of the enhanced focus and well-developed intent skills this experience gives. A healer with these abilities is termed a *skilled advanced healer*. Skilled advanced healers eventually discover that the art of giving Reiki is a mental exercise, one where Reiki—*powerful Reiki*—can be given anywhere around the world by simply quieting the mind, then through intent alone, *allowing* Reiki energy to flow to the client. It is not necessary to know where the client happens to be because the strength of their intent automatically provides the address of the client—all that is needed is the client's first name. Intent alone sends the healing energy to the right person involved.

Healers at this level no longer struggle to send Reiki with an agenda, that is, sending it for a particular purpose to an identified client. Such healers know that the Reiki they send will perform whatever healing is possible within the limitations of the client's incarnational plan and the essential limitations brought on by the biological condition of the body.

There is no shortcut or instruction set that can teach energy healing at this level. This is an esoteric skill that is brought about by constant study and use. A typical healing session is simple. The client or an agent for the client approaches the healer and asks for a healing. The healer, if willing to send Reiki at that time, asks for the first name of the client, then enters a quiet or meditative state and the Reiki energy begins to flow.

The healer will know right away if the Reiki is being accepted. If it is not accepted, the healer will inform the agent that he is not able to help at that time and the session is ended. Otherwise, the healer will spend as much time as is necessary for the healing to begin to take place. This can range from a few minutes to perhaps as long as a half hour.

A skilled advanced healer can also heal by using a combination of Reiki and empathic methods or by empathic methods alone. As can be imagined, such healers have a certain aura about them and visitors will know right away that they are in front of a special individual. Such healers generally aren't talkative, and only the bare minimum chit-chat at the beginning of the session is entertained. These healers are not usually interested in how they were "found" or what the results of the healing session are. They already know.

Skilled advanced healers such as these are relatively uncommon. They don't advertise, but even so, at times they are nearly overwhelmed by many looking for a healing. Yet they seldom turn away anyone who finds them because healing has become their life's work and there is little time for anything else.

Appendix

When we say that we understand a group of natural phenomena, we mean that we have found a constructive theory that embraces them.
—Albert Einstein

Your Client Logbook

As a serious Reiki practitioner, you should maintain a log of every treatment that you offer. The purpose of this journal is to provide a solid description of what you did and felt during the session. Such a journal is important when it comes time to review your experiences.

Also, should any legal action ever come your way, at least you'll be able to show what was going on and what happened from a written record. The log is particularly important if you were treating an underage client. When this is the case, it is highly recommended that a parent or guardian be present throughout the session. Make sure to obtain names and contact information of those attending the session.

Your log should contain at least the following information:

1. Date and start time of the session.

2. Client name and perhaps contact information if you like.

3. Client request (stated briefly). You can record this item after your session has ended.

4. Notes on the session, especially detailed if there was some client anxiety, discomfort or something unusual took place.

5. Session end time.

A convenient way to keep your log is to copy blank forms on your printer, then keep the log in a 3-ring binder. You can easily keep two or three sessions per page. Your log book should be kept on file for at least seven years for IRS considerations.

NOTES ON THE INCARNATIONAL PLAN

We have noted that incarnationally, physical sickness is sometimes bound to a metaphysically inspired illness. When this happens, it is due to a life not moving in the incarnationally planned direction and blocks that result in some form of "illness" placed to guide us back on track. Sicknesses bound to an illness usually respond nicely to Reiki healing energy as the insight it brings clarifies the changes necessary to get back on track. Your client may or may not immediately recognize the metaphysical healing that took place.

This sounds like we are bound to follow a narrow pathway throughout life or become sick. Such is not the case at all. The incarnational plan is strategic, meaning that what is to be accomplished can be met through any number of different paths, none particularly better than another. We have the free choice of which pathway we want to follow.

So we are perfectly free to come into the physical already knowing from a young age what we want to do, such as being a pilot, a doctor or fashion designer. But this isn't locked in stone and depending on our individual incarnational plan, we are free to change to a different profession or line of work almost any time. This makes it is possible to get experience through many different lifestyles.

Of course, there are lives whose purpose is to stay in one profession for an entire lifetime, in which case blocks were instilled that prevent freedom of professional choice. But other plans recognize that there are many ways the desired learning can take place and change is totally allowed or even encouraged.

We must remember that we were the co-authors of our incarnational plan and that it is we who gave it approval prior to us coming into this world. As such, the incarnational plan is a perfect match for each of us and us alone. But planning in the nonphysical cannot anticipate everything that can happen in this world. And so there are many "gaps" in the plan, some purposeful, others not, that allow changes in how and what we are doing.

Our incarnational plans, for the most part, are set up to present opportunities to accomplish a particular learning. If a learning opportunity is grasped and the learning accomplished, the plan starts setting up the next lesson.

But if the learning lessons are continually rejected, eventually we run out of "freedom of choice" options and the plan starts asserting itself, gently at first by presenting choices that will lead us back on track. And if we refuse these offerings, illness is often the result, illness that can range from loss of job, family or fortune to a serious medical condition. By running unchecked through bad choices, from the physical point of view, the incarnational plan can become quite brutal.

And so this is an instance where the healer can make a difference. Once our healing insight takes hold and is grasped by our client, a new perspective takes over and as the incarnational blocks are removed healing begins to take place. In this way, life for the client reaches out in whatever direction is best suited for that particular person.

THE SERPENT POWER: CHAKRA ENERGY HISTORY

The chakra energy system developed in India describes the various nonphysical energy centers and energy flows throughout the physical human body. In the Indian tradition, such centers are said to be inside the "subtle" body, the equivalent of our "collective consciousness," the sum of all the nonphysical bodies. Although other cultures describe human energy systems in a more or less similar fashion, India's chakra system is the best organized and documented and is the predominant system studied today.

The chakra system is complex. First written mention of these systems comes in the Vedas, the oldest written traditions in India. These texts were compiled by the Aryans, Indo-European invaders from the north of India. Assembled between roughly 2000 to 600 BCE, they also formed the basis of the Hindu religion.

The Vedas are considered to be divine revelations, which in the orthodox Hindu tradition are "heard," rather than seen or discovered in other ways. Medicine and healing are the two most important physical sciences explored and developed by these texts. Ayurveda, India's traditional medical system, Hatha yoga, Siddha yoga, Tantra philosophy and other yoga systems all find their roots in the Vedas.

The anatomy sections of various yoga systems extensively deal with so-called "modern" concepts such as embryology and heredity, but most importantly for this discussion, they also establish the foundation of metaphysical energy in the body and thoroughly explore its diffusion through the nervous system, basing it on chakra-linked energy management.

The first known mention of chakras as psychic centers of conscious awareness is in the *Yoga Sutras of Patanjali* of roughly 200 BCE and the *Yoga Upanishads* written around 600 CE. The chakras and Kundalini (energy flow) eventually came to be a part of yoga philosophy in the tantric tradition starting sometime between 200 BCE and 7 CE.

The entire concept of the chakras and related energy flow came to the West through a single book, Arthur Avalon's *The Serpent Power* first published in 1919. It contains his commentary and translation of the *Padaka-Pancaka* (of roughly the tenth century) describing the chakra centers and various practices related to them, and the *Sta-Cakra-Nirupana* (1577 CE). Chakra meditation practices are described in another book, the *Gorakshashatakam*, also from around the tenth century. Little has been added to this body of knowledge since that time.

These texts form the basis of the Western understanding of chakra theory and Kundalini yoga today. They are not light reading, and the knowledge is esoteric. Were it not for author Avalon's commentaries, they would be incomprehensible without the help of a guru to give meanings to the verses. Happily, for those with an interest, *The Serpent Power* (ISBN 0-486-23058-9) is available as an inexpensive reprint.

READING AND OTHER RESOURCES

1. *Aura-Reiki*, by Bill Waites, ISBN 965494107-4. This inexpensive book gives a complete explanation of the chakras and auras. Waites began his Reiki experience in India, and his views naturally reflect this influence on the practice. Well-written and highly detailed, this book is valuable as both a practical study guide and an introduction to his version of Reiki philosophy.

2. *The Chemistry of Conscious States*, by J. Allan Hobson, M.D., Professor of Psychiatry, Harvard Medical School, ISBN 0-316-36754-0. A gentle look at how consciousness evolves in the minds of dreamers, psychotics, and individuals under the influence of drugs. A good primer on the theory of human consciousness in general. Hobson has published several other books related to the brain in various states.

3. *Clear Creek Crystal Mine*, 60 Mary's Eagle Trail, Mount Ida, AR 71957; stu@arcrystalmine.com. One of many good places to buy inexpensive AAA fine crystals either singly or by the pound.

4. *The Dawn of Civilization* by G. Maspero. Published in 1894 (ISBN 9781162622309) and now available as a reprint, this classic book of 800 pages on Egyptian and Chaldean civilizations contains significant references to Sa (energy) and how it was given to those seeking healings.

5. *The Edwin Smith Surgical Papyrus*, James Henry Breasted (Editor), 638 pages. (Page count and price varies depending on the particular publisher chosen.) ISBN 1-162-92433-0. Several publications of this book are available. Translations of the papyrus are also available in variable quality from numerous sources on the web. This papyrus is described as "the most important document in the history of science surviving from the pre-Greek age (seventeenth century BCE)." Both to the medical profession and to the lay reader, the *Surgical Papyrus* will be of intense interest. It contains, for example, for the first time in human speech a word for

'brain.' Repeatedly the surgeon discusses cases of injured people some of whom he has no hope of saving.

6. *The Empath* (episode 61 of the original Star Trek series) shows with reasonable accuracy classic empathic healing. Although empaths of this particular nature and the healing power portrayed are seldom encountered today, it makes an entertaining story, even when the futuristic setting is ignored.

7. Fr. Thomas Keating's various writings and *The Spiritual Journey* (a video series) combines Christian spirituality with Ken Wilbur's concepts in a most interesting way. Of special interest, if you wish to start your adventure in this direction, are Keating's lectures in *The Spiritual Journey* tapes, part 2: The Human Condition: Evolutionary Model; Formation of the Homemade Self; Existential Model; and The Pre-rational Energy Centers. Visit Contemplative Outreach at http://www.contemplativeoutreach.org for information on his books and videos.

8. How natural healers often work is accurately depicted with just a little artistic license in the 1980s movie *Resurrection*, starring Ellen Burstyn. It is a beautiful and moving story describing the birth of a natural healer following a serious auto accident. Entertaining and enjoyable for everyone with an interest in healing, it shows some of the rejection that healers can face. It has an especially poignant and happy ending.

9. *Joy's Way* by W. Brugh Joy, M.D., ISBN 0-87477-085-8. A map for the transformational Journey: An introduction to the potentials for healing with body energies. Brugh's story of a miraculous healing and an illuminating meditation involving the chakra system, meditation and higher levels of consciousness.

10. *Molecules of Emotion* by Candace B. Pert, ISBN-10 0684846349. This book describes her research and discoveries of the opiate receptors of neural stimulants secreted by the body, as well as their effect on the mind. She also relates her experiences and collisions with the established medical community.

11. Our spiritual evolution from the anthropological perspective is eloquently expressed in Ken Wilbur's book, *Up from Eden* (ISBN 0-394-71424-5). It describes the various evolutionary phases of human mind development and their effect on society. Combined with Fr. Keating's work described above, it shows how we pass through those same evolutionary phases during our mental development from an infant to a fully grown adult. It reveals the deep and hidden contours, drives and motives behind our subconscious minds, and is a good foundation from which healers can better understand the human beings they heal.

12. *The Placebo Effect*, Walter A. Brown: *Scientific American*, January 1988. An in-depth, scientifically sound description of several blind tests of the placebo effect.

13. *The Power of Reiki* by Tanmaya Honervogt, ISBN 978-0-8050-5559-7 gives a complete traditional description of Reiki. Beautifully illustrated, this book is handed out as a part of my Reiki 1 classes. A newer second edition, ISBN 1250049482, is available on Amazon for less than $20.

14. There are many methods for increasing awareness and training the mind. Several programs that are available use audio techniques as mentioned in chapter 2. Two of them are the Monroe Institute (www.monroeinst.org) and *Centerpointe Research Institute* (www.centerpointe.com) products. Samples of each of these products can be downloaded at no cost.

15. *The Temple of Man: Apet of the South at Luxor* by R. A. Schwaller De Lubicz, ISBN 0-89281-570-1. This massive tome of some 1,055 pages, based on fifteen years of study at Luxor, deeply explores the Egyptian civilization which is surprisingly advanced and complex, more so than most recognize today. Deeply philosophical and based on the author's own personal exploration, this two-volume book set is costly. But it is of immense value to those searching for humanity's roots, early hints of the healer's practice and its spiritual foundation.

16. *The Uncommon Touch, An Investigation of Spiritual Healing* by Tom Harpur (ISBN 0-7710-2946-8). The author, a former religious editor for Canada's *Toronto Star* and a widely published columnist, describes many different healers and the effects they experience in their work in this most readable book. The techniques used by the healers he describes vary widely. A must-read book for everyone interested in energy healing.

INDEX

CPSIA information can be obtained
at www.ICGtesting.com
Printed in the USA
BVHW092332010223
657620BV00008B/924

9 780999 150757